# THE QUEEN'S NECKLACE

# Borgo Press Plays by ALEXANDRE DUMAS

*Anthony*
*The Count of Monte Cristo, Part One: The Betrayal of Edmond Dantès*
*The Count of Monte Cristo, Part Two: The Resurrection of Edmond Dantès*
*The Count of Monte Cristo, Part Three: The Rise of Monte Cristo*
*The Count of Monte Cristo, Part Four: The Revenge of Monte Cristo*
*A Fairy Tale* (with Adolphe de Leuven and Léon Lhérie)
*The Last of the Three Musketeers; or, The Prisoner of the Bastille* (Musketeers #3)
*The Three Musketeers—Twenty Years Later* (Musketeers #2)
*Napoléon Bonaparte*
*Richard Darlington*
*The San Felice*
*Sylvandire*
*The Three Musketeers* (Musketeers #1)
*The Two Dianas*
*Urbain Grandier and the Devils of Loudon*
*The Venetian*
*The Whites and the Blues*
*Young Louix XIV*

RELATED DRAMAS:

*The Queen's Necklace*, by Pierre Decourcelle
*The Son of Porthos the Musketeer*, by Émile Blavet (Musketeers #4)
*A Summer Night's Dream*, by Adolphe de Leuven and Joseph-Bernard Rosier
*The Widow's Husband; and, Porthos in Search of an Outfit: Two Dumasian Comedies* (Frank J. Morlock, editor)

# THE QUEEN'S NECKLACE

## A PLAY IN FIVE ACTS

## PIERRE DECOURCELLE

Adapted from the Novel by Alexandre Dumas
Translated by Frank J. Morlock

THE BORGO PRESS
MMXII

*For Carmen Martínez*

# CONTENTS

# CAST OF CHARACTERS

King Louis XVI
Cardinal de Rohan
Cagliostro
Beausire
The Portuguese
Bossange
De Charny
Saint Landry
Reteau de Villette
Ducorneau
Count d'Artois
Count de Provence
Bailli de Suffren
De Breteuil
Bohemer
Gamain
De Crussol
De Coigny
De Calonne
De Besenal
De Vangriul
L'Artaigne
Marat
The Philosopher
De Polastron
A Porter

Le Positif
Le Griqneux
De Souz
The Commander
Queen Marie Antoinette
Oliva
Countess de la Motte-Valois
Duchess de Polignac
Andrea de Taverney
Princess de Lamballe
Madame Campan
Countess de Challons
Countess de Polastron
Countess de Coigny
Nicolette
Araminth
Dame Clothilde
Nina
Sylvia
Philomena
Amaranth
Zephyr
Clelie
Rosalie
Ypsibee
Hyacinth
Corinne
Countess de Grammont
Madame de Sabran
Coresondra
Cydalise
Clorinda
Madame de Beauvilliers
Madame de Deux-Ponts

# ACT I

## SCENE 1: DAUGHTER OF KINGS

*A dilapidated room in a furnished hotel of the lowest sort, in the Hotel de Reims, Rue de la Verrerie. On the wall, a portrait—of a long, pale bearded face—pointed beard, cap on head, ruffle at his throat—with this inscription: Henry of Valois. Chimney in which smokes the wretched remains of a log.*

COUNTESS de la MOTTE

(alone, seated at a table, writing) "In the hope that you will indeed continue your kindness to me, deign to accept, Madame la Duchess, the very respectful homage of your very humble and devoted servant, Jeanne de Saint Rémy, Countess de la Motte-Valois."

What can be hoped from such humiliation?

(she reads the addresses of her letters) Madame la Duchess de Polignac, favorite of the Queen—ten crowns—Madame Compan, first lady attending Her Majesty—three crowns—Mr. de Breteuil, minister of state—an audience. Mr. de Calonée—advise—Mr. de Cagliostro—five crowns, for he's often given me. They still say that he makes gold. It's true he promised me a visit, on which, if I am clever and determined, my destiny will depend. Clever, I am. As for determination, misery will give us some.

(knocking) Come in!

(Beausire enters.)

COUNTESS de la MOTTE

Heavens, Mr. Beausire, my neighbor on the same floor. What can I do for you, Mr. de Beausire?

BEAUSIRE

Imagine that yesterday at my academy, after a series of unexpected blows in the depths of a gaming house, my belt broke,— so much so that for supper, I had to pawn my cloak—there, Countess, see my dress.

(he turns and points to an immense hole) And I was counting on your assistance.

COUNTESS de la MOTTE

Alas, my poor Beausire, I am as short of money as you.

BEAUSIRE

Is that possible? You, a descendant of the Valois, a daughter of kings. Come! I shall hold my hat like this—

(he makes a comic effort) —to hide my hole. Ah! We wouldn't be reduced to this begging if Oliva had not left me.

COUNTESS de la MOTTE

Your unfaithful one! Who abandoned you at break of day when I moved in beside you. So you still regret her?

BEAUSIRE

Yes, I regret her! The perfidious one! But, Oliva, Madame, she was the song of my life, the bird in my cage, the sun in my sky. We argued, we insulted each other, we fought—but the candle went out, hell became a paradise! And to say that she left, on her birthday—left over a wretched flower pot.

COUNTESS de la MOTTE

That you had forgotten to give her?

BEAUSIRE

No, that I broke over her head.

COUNTESS de la MOTTE

Plague, cousin! You are not going to get there by striking hard.

BEAUSIRE

Ah! Madame. Does love exist without jealousy?

COUNTESS de la MOTTE

And this Oliva gave you a topic on which to exercise yours?

BEAUSIRE

On the first of January at Saint Silvester—Great Lords, the tax farmers, officers, priests, even lawyers all were good to her. The last month I surprised her with a bailiff in my dressing gown.

COUNTESS de la MOTTE

What did she say?

BEAUSIRE

She insisted he had seized it. And the fact is he did seize it! But I won't importune you any more, Countess. I am going to make a tour of the Palace Royal—the devil will indeed be in it if I don't hunt out a pair of pistoles. And perhaps I'll have some news of my traitress.

COUNTESS de la MOTTE

Good luck, Mr. Beausire!

BEAUSIRE

Ah, Madame, no—there's what it is to give flowers to women— it brings bad luck.

(He leaves.)

COUNTESS de la MOTTE

Let's see—let's resume our accounts. Total 10 crowns and I promised twenty to Mr. de la Motte to help him support his garrison at Montmedy. Poor devil—our marriage has not enriched him.

(ringing, she calls) Clothilde! Clothilde! They're ringing! Are you going to hurry?

CLOTHILDE

On my way.

(She leaves.)

COUNTESS de la MOTTE

If it were the visit Mr. Cagliostro announced to me—

(she pushes her papers into a drawer and throws herself in an armchair)

ANDREA

(at the door on the landing) Does the Countess de la Motte Valois dwell here?

CLOTHILDE

Yes, Madame.

ANDREA

(to another lady who is not in view) You can come in, Madame, she's here.

CLOTHILDE

Who shall I announce to the Countess?

ANDREA

Announce two ladies of Good Deeds—

CLOTHILDE

From Paris?

QUEEN

No, from Versailles.

(Clothilde introduces the Queen and Andrea de Taverney—who are very muffled up in their furs. Clothilde leaves. The Countess advances two armchairs and bows to her visitors, designating seats to them.)

ANDREA

They told us about your situation, Countess, things which interested us, Madame and myself, and we wanted to have some details about things which concern you.

COUNTESS de la MOTTE

Ladies, you see the portrait of Henry II, my ancestor, for I am truly of the blood of Valois. As to the rest, if you are pleased to question me, I am prepared to respond to you.

ANDREA

They told us your father is dead?

COUNTESS de la MOTTE

Yes, Madame, my father, the Count de Saint-Rémy, born of Valois, great-grandson of Henry II, died in poverty and from starvation.

ANDREA

Is it possible? Died here?

COUNTESS de la MOTTE

Not even here, in the poor hovel, not in his bed—that bed was a pallet! My father died side by side with the most wretched and the most vile—my father died at the Hotel Dieu—in Paris!

ANDREA

Great God!

QUEEN

And your mother?

COUNTESS de la MOTTE

When my father married her, she was a rare beauty, but alas! Poverty helping, this beauty, was altered and with it, my mother's character. At the least fault, which would make another mother smile, mine would beat me. From the power of blows, she taught me a phrase that instinctively I did not want to retain—then she tossed me into the street with the order to recite it to the first passer-by—if I didn't want to be beaten to death.

ANDREA

Frightful! Frightful!

QUEEN

And what was this phrase?

COUNTESS de la MOTTE

Sir, take pity on a little orphan who's descended in a straight line from Henry II of Valois, King of France. The cold is making you shiver, Madame and I am in despair but wood has just risen to six pounds, which puts it at seventy pounds to the cord—and my store is exhausted.

QUEEN

It's not cold that's making me shiver, Madame—it's pity from listening to you. But can you furnish proof justifying your genealogy?

COUNTESS de la MOTTE

Here's what you desire, Madame.

(gives papers that the Queen examines)

QUEEN

(very kindly) You were right, Countess. These titles are perfectly in order—and with them you will no doubt obtain a pension for yourself, and an advancement for your husband. While waiting, the Office of Good Deeds authorizes me to offer you this slight assistance.

(She offers her a roll of coins.)

COUNTESS de la MOTTE

When shall I have the Honor of thanking you again?

QUEEN

We will let you know within a week because I promise you news from us, but it's beginning to get late, our sleigh is expecting us, and we must reach Versailles—come, Andrea!

COUNTESS de la MOTTE

Allow me, Miladies, to light you out.

(going to take the lamp from the table, she fingers the roll of coins) Crowns of a few pounds. Fifty or perhaps a hundred.

ANDREA

(putting herself together) Goodbye, Countess—and till soon—

(they leave)

COUNTESS de la MOTTE

Open, Clothilde—Miladies, I am your very humble servant.

(she makes a curtsy)

(weighing the roll) I'm not mistaken—only fifty crowns—

(she dumps the roll into a bronze cup on the table) What do I see—double crowns—fifty double crows—two thousand four hundred pounds—so these ladies are very rich! Oh! I'll find them again.

(she trips on a box) What's that? A candy box in gold—a woman's portrait—it resembles the larger of these ladies—no question, a mother or an ancestor—if they were still here.

(she opens a window) No! Still there's a chaise with porters in front of the house—but they spoke of a sleigh. Oh! How cold it is.

CLOTHILDE

Madame! Madame! It's another visit.

COUNTESS de la MOTTE

Yet another lady of charity?

CLOTHILDE

No, this time it's a gentleman. And he has a tremendously more distinguished air—he says that Madame wrote to him.

COUNTESS de la MOTTE

I wrote to everybody. But show him in quickly, Dame Clothilde.

(as the old woman goes to the door, aside) Come, Providence— yet another 100 crowns.

(a gesture of attention and uncertainty by the Countess on the quality of the visitor)

ROHAN

(entering) Madame Countess—I am Cardinal de Rohan.

COUNTESS de la MOTTE

Monsignor.

(she curtsies to him and designates an armchair)

ROHAN

My friend, the Count De Cagliostro told me of your misfortune and it is he who convinced me to pay you a visit.

COUNTESS de la MOTTE

(aside, meaningfully) Ah!

(aloud) It's a kindness for which I will be eternally grateful to him, Monsignor.

ROHAN

You are living alone?

COUNTESS de la MOTTE

Absolutely alone, Monsignor.

ROHAN

That's nice on the part of a young and pretty woman.

COUNTESS de la MOTTE

It's simple, Monsignor, on the part of a woman who would be displaced in all of the society except that into which her poverty carries her.

ROHAN

Madame, I hope that you are not at the end of your resources. You have property somewhere—which must be mortgaged. Family jewels.

(noticing the box on which the Countess is drumming her fingers) This one, for example—an original box—on my word—will you allow me, Madame?

(surprised) A portrait.

COUNTESS de la MOTTE

You seem to know the original of this painting, Monsignor?

ROHAN

No question! It's that of Marie-Therese.

COUNTESS de la MOTTE

(excited)

Maria-Therese, Empress of Austria. You think so, Monsignor.

ROHAN

I am certain of it. But where did you get this candy box, Madame?

COUNTESS de la MOTTE

From a Lady of Charity who came here just now with one of her friends, and who willingly promised me her protection, leaving a 100 crowns on my table.

ROHAN

Pardon, Countess, but could you give me a portrait of this generous donator?

COUNTESS de la MOTTE

My God, Monsignor, that would be difficult for me because this lady had her face hidden under an ample scarf.

ROHAN

But didn't she name her companion?

COUNTESS de la MOTTE

Indeed—once, by her baptismal name.

ROHAN

Which is?

COUNTESS de la MOTTE

Andrea—

ROHAN

(aside) Andrea de Taverney—the Queen! The Queen here! Indeed, these mysterious ramblings in Paris are indeed in her habits.

COUNTESS de la MOTTE

What's wrong with you, Monsignor, you seem very upset?

ROHAN

Say that I am happy, Countess, happy at the luck which is befalling you—because with the protectress you have conquered today, it is impossible that within a short time the whole world won't take an interest in you.

COUNTESS de la MOTTE

But this protectress?

ROHAN

Is called Marie-Antoinette, Archduchess of Austria, Queen of France.

COUNTESS de la MOTTE

The Queen—

ROHAN

(boldly) Yes, Countess, the Queen, who you certainly seduced and conquered as—

COUNTESS de la MOTTE

As—?

ROHAN

As you must seduce and conquer all those who have the privilege of approaching you—

COUNTESS de la MOTTE

(bitterly) Ah! Monsignor, ask valets who have escorted me out, chambermaids who kicked me out the door, Swiss who've given me my walking papers!

ROHAN

The nightmare is over, since the Queen is extending her tutelary hand to you—and, meanwhile, if you wish to do me a favor, you will not speak of accepting my protection—As God is not pleased that I utter this word which humiliates me more than you—but to consider me as a friend—devoted and sincere—I would regard myself as your obligee.

COUNTESS de la MOTTE

The offer is too delicately put to be rejected.

ROHAN

(kissing her hand) Then we are friends, it is signed—

COUNTESS de la MOTTE

It is sworn.

ROHAN

In that case, Countess, make me a promise?

COUNTESS de la MOTTE

What?

ROHAN

Friends pay each other visits, right? Promise me to return the one I have made you today?

COUNTESS de la MOTTE

Oh! Monsignor, you can't be thinking of it, for me to go to your hotel!

ROHAN

Soon you will be going to a minister's.

COUNTESS de la MOTTE

A minister is not a man, Monsignor Rohan—

ROHAN

You are adorable. Well, it's not a question of my hotel. I know a house—

COUNTESS de la MOTTE

(ironic) A small house—

ROHAN

No, Madame—a house—yours.

COUNTESS de la MOTTE

(coquettishly) Mine—and where's that? I don't know this house—

ROHAN

Would you allow me to show it to you this evening? And once you have seen it, would you do me the favor of inviting me to supper there?

COUNTESS de la MOTTE

(aside) Cagliostro—were you then speaking the truth?

(aloud) Ah! Monsignor, I was hoping that Your Eminence would deign to remember that if God has made me poor, he at least left me the pride of my rank.

ROHAN

See here, Countess, I will make you angry telling you that you are lodged in a manner little agreeable to a woman of your name. On the other hand, as a friend, you are granting me, I think the favor of seeing you sometimes. In a furnished hotel, my visits loan themselves to nasty remarks, to scandal; if you knew how mean they are to me—! And that's why I am asking of you the service of accepting the lodging I am offering you. You see, humiliation in all this?

COUNTESS de la MOTTE

Pardon, Monsignor, because you are forcing me to confess there does not exist a man more delicate than you.

ROHAN

(who has written in his notebook) Here's the address of your dwelling! I am placing it in this box.

(he considers the box and shuts the address in it) On the subject of this box, now that you know the name of your benefactress, you won't fail to return it to Her Majesty.

COUNTESS de la MOTTE

I won't fail.

ROHAN

Say there, Countess, once you've conquered the Queen, in your turn, you will protect me.

COUNTESS de la MOTTE

Near the Queen?

ROHAN

Alas, I am not in her good books.

(passionately) And that desolates me—because I would have given my life to—

COUNTESS de la MOTTE

To please her—

ROHAN

(stopping abruptly) To please her—yes, Countess—for one is not Prime Minister if one is not agreeable to Her Majesty.

COUNTESS de la MOTTE

Admit that it would be strange, all the same, Monsignor, if your portfolio was found in this little box.

ROHAN

What are you saying?

COUNTESS de la MOTTE

What would you make of me, Monsignor, if I made a Prime Minister of you?

ROHAN

What Cardinal de Bourbon made of Madame de Prie, his ally, his councilor, his associate, what a dream, Countess—two heads to govern France—two heads and a single heart!

COUNTESS de la MOTTE

Till soon—!

ROHAN

(kissing her hand) In your house.

COUNTESS de la MOTTE

(with a curtsy) Never shall I be such an ingrate, Monsignor, as to forget you arc at homc there.

(calling) Dame Clothilde, light out Monsignor.

CLOTHILDE

(with a torch, speechless and making a grotesque curtsy) Monsignor!

ROHAN

(aside, leaving) Let's go! This woman has too much wit not to capture the Queen as she has captured me.

(He leaves.)

COUNTESS de la MOTTE

(alone) Decidedly, I will end by believing sorcerers!

(to Clothilde, who returns) Come here, Dame Clothilde, and see!

(she shows her the gold in the bowl)

CLOTHILDE

Jesus, Holy Virgin, so much money!

COUNTESS de la MOTTE

You were worried about your wages.

CLOTHILDE

Oh, Madame, I never said that!

COUNTESS de la MOTTE

Here for your pay—and here's for the hotel—here's for the grocer—here's for the restaurant owner—

CLOTHILDE

Fine, Madame.

COUNTESS de la MOTTE

And now, run to Master Pingret, the second-hand clothes dealer and repurchase from him my beautiful trimmed gown, the last gift of that dear Madame de Beauvilliers, my benefactress, poor dress that I was obliged to put in pawn the day of her death, so as to be able to wear mourning.

CLOTHILDE

I'm hurrying there, Madame. Returning, I will purchase the

wherewithal to concoct Madame a nice little dinner.

COUNTESS de la MOTTE

(very haughtily) For whom do you take me? I don't dine, and I will never again dine in your wretched place.

(she leaves proudly)

CLOTHILDE

(alone) Ah! For sure she must have become rich suddenly to be as insolent as that.

(noises off) But one would say they're knocking at the door of Mr. de Beausire. And that voice! I'd swear that it was that of—

(she opens the door) Yes, indeed—Miss Oliva!

OLIVA

(gaily) You said it, respectable octogenarian.

CLOTHILDE

Why come in—will you—Mr. de Beausire has taken your key.

OLIVA

To come in here—It's that I am with someone.

(she points to Cagliostro, who appears in the doorway)

CLOTHILDE

The Count de Cagliostro!

OLIVA

Heavens, mother Methusalim, you know the Count?

CAGLIOSTRO

Am I not known by everybody? Dame Clothilde, would you watch on Mr. de Beausire's landing and introduce him here when you see him?

(Exit Clothilde.)

OLIVA

You can't think of it! Put Beausire face to face with you—he will kill you.

CAGLIOSTRO

(very calm) My dear Miss Oliva—when I met you a week ago in the Palace-Royal, I placed at your feet a refuge against Mr. Beausire and his flower pots. Have I kept my word?

OLIVA

As to that, yes—

CAGLIOSTRO

During that week, in like manner, clothing, nourishment—have you had all that you wish?

OLIVA

And even more. I've never eaten so well in my life!

CAGLIOSTRO

You will grant me that I have not for a moment forgotten the respect that I owe you.

OLIVA

Oh! God! Not one poor little time! To the degree it was ungracious! Ah! One might say that if one eats well at your place, you have no appetite.

CAGLIOSTRO

My dear child, the moment has come for us to explain ourselves plainly.

OLIVA

Oof! That will please me!

CAGLIOSTRO

What do you do all day?

OLIVA

I do nothing.

CAGLIOSTRO

You are lazy—very well? Do you like to stroll?

OLIVA

A lot.

CAGLIOSTRO

To attend spectacles, balls—?

OLIVA

Always.

CAGLIOSTRO

To live well?

OLIVA

Especially.

CAGLIOSTRO

If I gave twenty-five or fifty crowns a month what would you say?

OLIVA

I would prefer fifty to twenty-five, but what must I do to earn them?

CAGLIOSTRO

You will receive me in your home, you will give me your arm when I ask for it, you will await me when I tell you—

OLIVA

All that is not impossible to arrange.

CAGLIOSTRO

Perhaps I'll need for you to really be my mistress.

OLIVA

Oh, sir, trust me, you'll never need that.

CAGLIOSTRO

Or at least that you seem so.

OLIVA

As for that, as much as you like.

CAGLIOSTRO

Then it's agreed. Here's the first month in advance.

OLIVA

And here's Beausire—get out!

CAGLIOSTRO

Me—why?

OLIVA

Do you hear how he's screaming—ah! So much the worse for you if some misfortune happens.

CAGLIOSTRO

(sitting peacefully) How you talk! So much the worse!

BEAUSIRE

(entering furious) By the horns of Beelzebub! Where is he, this fox—so I can gut him so—so I can disembowel him, so I can cut him to shreds!

OLIVA

My friend!

BEAUSIRE

(brutally) You! Try to shut up!

CAGLIOSTRO

There! There! Don't be so rough to Madame, Monsieur de Beausire, and if you're in a bad mood!

BEAUSIRE

Death of all the devils in hell—get up and leave or I'll break this armchair and everything in it.

CAGLIOSTRO

(very calm) You didn't tell me, Miss, that Mr. de Beausire had these violent whims. Zounds! What ferocity!

BEAUSIRE

(exasperated, pulling his rapier) One more time, get up or I'll nail you to the back of the chair.

CAGLIOSTRO

(pulling a long sword) Really—try it!

OLIVA

Help!

CAGLIOSTRO

(still seated, sword in hand) Child, shush or you will make Mr. de Beausire deaf and that will make him skewer himself.

BEAUSIRE

(already on guard, stopping) Skewer myself? You said skewer myself—

CAGLIOSTRO

Like a chicken or a turkey at your choice.

BEAUSIRE

(sheathing his sword) Then if you are sure of it, admit it would be stupid of me to risk such an alternative.

CAGLIOSTRO

(sheathing also) If you had let me speak, I would have calmed your wrath with a single word.

BEAUSIRE

Which is?

CAGLIOSTRO

(deftly) I am Miss's uncle.

BEAUSIRE

Her uncle! She never told me she had one.

CAGLIOSTRO

That's because I was in the New World.

OLIVA

(entering into his idea) Oh, Uncle had left when I was so tiny, tiny that I'd almost forgotten about him.

BEAUSIRE

Ah, bah! Why then you are an uncle from America?

CAGLIOSTRO

You've guessed it.

BEAUSIRE

Oh! Why then that considerably changes the look of things.

(uneasily) By the way—did you return from there rich?

CAGLIOSTRO

Too rich to know my fortune! I have more money than I want.

BEAUSIRE

I really was saying so—that changes things at all at all—but I'm thinking—if you are my wife's uncle—you're also mine! In my arms—uncle!

CAGLIOSTRO

What do you think?

(during the embrace Oliva offers her hand to Cagliostro, who kisses it. After that Cagliostro pulls Beausire to him) By the way, nephew, aren't you a member of a certain academy?

BEAUSIRE

Me?

CAGLIOSTRO

Oh! Don't protest, I am not speaking of the Academy Française, but of a fraternity of Pharo cards, 21, and other analogous diversions which hold sessions in Rue de Vert-Bois—near to Porte-Saint Martin—upstairs over the ground floor—

BEAUSIRE

Keep it down!—Well?

CAGLIOSTRO

Well! In a quarter of an hour, at your academy they're going to discuss a little pending project to give a benefice of nearly 2 million pounds to its associates.

BEAUSIRE

Head and blood! Why, if I'm not there, I'll lose my share.

COUNTESS de la MOTTE

(enters in high fashion, with arms uncovered) You, my dear Count?

CAGLIOSTRO

Myself, Countess! But how beautiful you are!

(kissing her hand) Ah! I understand the visit took place—and no doubt you are going to dine—with him!

COUNTESS de la MOTTE

Can one hide nothing from a sorcerer! Why, it's Mr. Beausire— oh! How happy you seem.

BEAUSIRE

There's something to it, Countess. I found her again.

(he unmasks Oliva, who curtsies, the Countess recoils stupe- fied)

COUNTESS de la MOTTE

(not taking her eyes from Oliva) Huh? Madame is Miss Oliva—

OLIVA

To serve you, Madame.

COUNTESS de la MOTTE

(still watching her) I understand—the joy of Mr. Beausire, Miss, as I now am able to explain to myself all his past sorrow—

(curtsy by Oliva; aside) Oh, this resemblance is truly terrifying.

CAGLIOSTRO

(low) What's the matter with you, Countess?

COUNTESS de la MOTTE

(hiding her emotion) Me—nothing.

CAGLIOSTRO

You find this girl resembles her—huh?

COUNTESS de la MOTTE

Resembles whom?

CAGLIOSTRO

(taking the candy box on the table, still low) Well, if not to the original, at least to the owner of this portrait. But here's Dame Clothilde who, no question, is coming to inform you that your carriage awaits you. Good luck, Countess. You are grasping fortune, don't let it go!

COUNTESS de la MOTTE

(putting on the cloak the old woman holds for her) Have confidence in me.

(to Oliva) Goodbye! I hope to see you again, Miss.

(aside) Oh! It is impossible that God in making such a prodigy has not had his plans!

CAGLIOSTRO

That's my opinion!

(aside) But we will assist them.

**CURTAIN**

# ACT I

## SCENE 2: THE PORT
## SAINT MARTIN IN 1784

*The stage represents the square of boulevards and the Rue Saint Martin in 1784. In the rear, the Saint Martin gate and the Faubourg in perspective, all white with snow—to the right and to the left, the boulevards—and on each side the sides of the houses forming the corner of the Rue Saint Martin. To the left, the shop of the locksmith Gamain, "Locksmith to His Majesty". In front of this shop a large pyramid of snow and ice, surmounted by busts of the King and Queen, decorated with ribbons and surrounded by a cordon of illuminated lanterns. Further back, to the left, a house whose door is usable. In the house on the right is found the basement entrance to the Academy of Beausire. In front of the Gate of Saint Martin two large illuminated braziers around which a population of beggars warm themselves and who line up to get to it. Three street lamps—one in the middle of the street. The two others on each side of the boulevards and the Gate of Saint Martin.*

*At Rise, on the steps and stools, workers, shopkeepers put the last touches to the pyramid on the left and light lanterns.*

WORKERS

Long live Master Gamain!

GAMAIN

Who's placed the busts of the king and queen on his obelisk) There—here's our work finished, Mr. Ducorneau.

PERINE

Oh! How good it looks!

DUCORNEAU

Truly, Master Gamain, you are surpassing yourself in the erection of this obelisk. Just now, returning from the Portuguese Embassy where I had the honor of being chancellor, I was admiring that of the Rue Coq-Saint-Honoré since it is the fashion in Paris to test our gratitude to our sovereigns with such monuments, but it is eclipsed by yours.

GAMAIN

Then you think that my royal pupil will be satisfied with me?

DUCORNEAU

Transported. Indeed, you are teaching locksmithing to our monarch, one would say he profits handsomely from your lessons.

SAINT-LANDRY

(arriving unexpectedly) By Jove! With a master like Mr. Gamain?

GAMAIN

There's that bad lot. It's Landry, my old clerk. I thought you got rich while waiting to be hanged.

SAINT-LANDRY

Rich, yes, master. I have been indeed. I even had a lackey and was called the Chevalier de Saint Landry—but this cursed winter has ruined my business.

GAMAIN

Really? What business are you in, Mr. Wiseguy?

SAINT-LANDRY

I keep, with a few honest friends of mine, a place of recreation where certain persons of good company come to relax from the fatigues of the day by playing a few games of cards.

GAMAIN

Meaning, you govern a gambling hall where you fleece imbeciles.

SAINT-LANDRY

Fleece! Fie! Curry nothing more! But alas! For the last three months—the pigeons—I mean the amateurs no longer venture out at night for fear of being frozen or breaking their necks on the ice and so I've had to make economies.

GAMAIN

You are croaking of hunger.

SAINT-LANDRY

Oh! Not at all! I have a profession.

GAMAIN

Beggar.

SAINT-LANDRY

No! Run over! Yes, an idea came to me after the last frost. I watch for carriages or the sleighs slipping at high speed on the boulevards, and as soon as one passes having the appearance to me of being rich, I beat on the snow with howls to break your soul. They flock around, they stop my road hog. They pick me up, limping as low as I can. The unfortunate is crippled, yelps an old woman. Yie! Yie! And I limp lower still. For life, perhaps—my moneybag fumbles in his pocket—and the trick is played. The next day with a dancing girl from the Opera, I limp through 15 crowns, let the winter be harsh for two more months and I'll be a landlord.

GAMAIN

But if the thaw comes, you will end in the galleys of the King. As to the rest, I predicted it to you.

DUCORNEAU

(who comes to admire the obelisk) By the way, neighbor, our monument lacks an inscription. The one at the Coq Saint Honoré has one in verse rhymed by Mr. Marmontel in person.

GAMAIN

It's Mr. Reteau de Villette, a news manager of my clients, who took charge of ours. Precisely—here's our author.

RETEAU

(enters with an apprentice holding a painted poster) Everything's ready to put your inscription in place, Master Gamain.

GAMAIN

Let's see it.

RETEAU

Here—it's a quatrain:

Queen whose beauty surpasses all others
Take your place here next to a beneficent king
If the edifice is of snow and ice, frail!
Our hearts for you will endure.

DUCORNEAU

Ah! Bravo!

THE PEOPLE

(who are grouped around) Yes, bravo!

SAINT-LANDRY

To me the glory of hanging it.

(he hangs it)

GAMAIN

Your quatrain is very fine, Mr. Reteau! Still, as a notable of this quarter, I would have wished it a bit longer.

RETEAU

Next time, Gamain, I'll do it double for you.

DUCORNEAU

Brr! The cold increases. Gentlemen, in my capacity as chancellor of the Portuguese Embassy, I receive excellent wine from Oporto—I am making you the offer of a bottle to the health of our sovereign.

GAMAIN

With joy! I will tell this tomorrow to Louis, it will please him.

DUCORNEAU

Louis? Who's that, Louis?

GAMAIN

Well, Louis XVI, my apprentice.

(They go into Ducorneau's.)

SAINT-LANDRY

(alone) Let's see, I've received in the name of our president, a invitation for this evening.

L'ARTAIGNE

(appearing abruptly) And I, too, my dear Landry.

POSITIVE

It's like mine.

THE PHILOSOPHER

And me, too!

SAINT-LANDRY

(shaking hands) Hello, L'Artaigne—Hello, Philosopher—Hello, Positive—do you suspect what our President can have to communicate to us?

THE PORTUGUESE

(appearing) I am going to tell you, gentlemen. And first of all, excuse me for having convoked you in the middle of street despite the cold. But as discreet as a cabaret or an inn may be, the owner prowls about, a waiter listens and what I have to tell you demands the most rigorous secrecy. But are we all here?

SAINT-LANDRY

I insist above all, if it's a question of an operation that those absent lose their share.

BEAUSIRE

(appearing suddenly) Me, too.

ALL

Beausire.

BEAUSIRE

In person—you weren't expecting me, it seems? And the gentleman whose teeth are longer than his waist was going to steal my share of the cake that I was getting prepared to eat!

SAINT-LANDRY

Sir!

BEAUSIRE

Sir!

(puts his hand on his sword!

THE PORTUGUESE

(duly) Enough, no quarrels! And before we fight over the chestnuts let's pull them from the fire.

THE PHILOSOPHER

He's right.

POSITIVE

That's positive!

L'ARTAIGNE

What's it all about?

ALL

Yes, what?

THE PORTUGUESE

Have you heard tell of the Diamond Necklace of Mssrs. Boehmer and Bossage?

SAINT-LANDRY

The famous necklace of 16 hundred thousand pounds?

BEAUSIRE

That Her Majesty the Queen refused?

SAINT-LANDRY

Saying that France had greater need of a ship of the line than the Queen of new diamonds.

THE PORTUGUESE

Precisely, well, as for me, I've found another Queen to make the purchase.

THE ASSOCIATES

And that's?

THE PORTUGUESE

(removing his hat) She's my gracious sovereign the Queen of Portugal)

BEAUSIRE

I confess I don't understand.

SAINT-LANDRY

Nor I! For once we're in agreement.

THE PORTUGUESE

It's really quite simple, for the moment, the Embassy of Portugal is vacant. There's an interim The new ambassador, Mr. de Souza, for family reasons, won't arrive in Paris for a few months.

SAINT-LANDRY

Well?

THE PORTUGUESE

Well—what's to prevent this ambassador from arriving, sooner and installing himself.

BEAUSIRE

You want—

THE PORTUGUESE

And if this ambassador wants a necklace for his sovereign doesn't he have the right to purchase it?

SAINT-LANDRY

I understand.

ALL

Me too.

THE PORTUGUESE

The hotel is occupied only by a grotesque Chancellor, Mr. Ducorneau, who speaks Portuguese the way I do Arabic. In the Chancellry there is a cash box. We will empty it like an account in the hand of jewelers. Moreover, we will demand their correspondent in Lisbon, and we will sign them, seal them, stamp them, with as many bills of exchange as they wish on this correspondent.

BEAUSIRE

One of them comes to receive them by bringing the necklace.

SAINT-LANDRY

(in a meaningful tone) And during the voyage, a jeweler goes to heaven and a million in our pockets.

THE PHILOSOPHER, POSITIVE, L'ARTAIGNE

Admirable.

THE PORTUGUESE

So then, gentlemen, you adopt my idea?

ALL

Unanimously.

BEAUSIRE

When will it be executed?

THE PORTUGUESE

I will warn you as soon as the moment comes, for it will require time to prepare everything. Until then, God keep you—are you coming, Mr. Beausire?

BEAUSIRE

Yes, I will accompany you to Bancelin's where I'm having a family dinner.

SAINT-LANDRY

(timidly, stopping the Portuguese) Pardon.

THE PHILOSOPHER

(likewise) But while awaiting the action.

L'ARTAIGNE

(likewise) Couldn't you?

SAINT-LANDRY

(extending his hand) Advance us—

POSITIVE

That's positive.

THE PORTUGUESE

(proudly) Ah! gentlemen! Don't you know the proud Motto of Portugal: Always borrow! Never pay.

(he exits slowly followed by the others who vainly try to soften him)

(The beggars continue to warm themselves at the braziers in the back, but more scattered. Cagliostro enters from the left and examines the obelisk.)

RETEAU

(in his doorway at the left) Goodbye, dear Mr. Ducorneau, and thanks for your politeness—

(he raises the collar of his cloak) Brrr! The cold is going to bite tonight.

CAGLIOSTRO

(bowing) Pardon! Is it indeed Mr. Reteau de Villette that I have the honor of addressing?

RETEAU

(returning the bow) Himself.

CAGLIOSTRO

Mr. Reteau de Villette, author of this quatrain that my lock-smith, Master Gamain told me of?

RETEAU

Indeed.

CAGLIOSTRO

And author at the same time, amongst the works of the same sort, of this last opus. The Seraglio of the Austrian, or the debauchs of Antoinette, whose anonymous author was condemned to row for ten years in the King's galleys?

RETEAU

Sir—

CAGLIOSTRO

Oh! Don't worry, I am not on the side of Mr. de Crosne's police—and I know what supreme and mysterious order you obeyed in writing praise as well as the pamphlet—

RETEAU

You know—who are you?

CAGLIOSTRO

(in a deep solemn tone) I am the one who is—

RETEAU

And where are you coming from?

COUNTESS de la MOTTE

(the same) I am coming from the country—where the light

comes from.

RETEAU

Is it possible? You could be the one that all of us, the most low, the most great of our association—we're ordered to expect soon.

CAGLIOSTRO

Is there a recognition sign by which the lowest and the great, you must recognize him?

RETEAU

He will bear on his breast a plaque of diamonds on which will shine three letters—the true first letters of the slogan which is the principal of our work—P.L.D.—Pedibus lilia destrue.

CAGLIOSTRO

Trample the lilies underfoot.

(he opens his cloak and on his breast over his heart shines a plaque with three letters in diamonds)

RETEAU

(very respectful) The Grand Master.

CAGLIOSTRO

My brother, you remember the oath taken by you at the moment you were admitted as one of us?

RETEAU

(with somber fanaticism) In the name of the crucified God, I swear to break the fleshly links that attach me to father, mother, brothers, sisters, relatives, friends, mistresses, kings, benefactors and all beings whatsoever to whom I've promised faith, obedience, or services saving the Grand Master to whom I belong, heart, body, soul and thought.

CAGLIOSTRO

That's fine.

RETEAU

Master, pardon me, but your words, your presence in this country seem to indicate that the struggle awaited by our 3 million brothers is on the point of commencing.

CAGLIOSTRO

Yes.

RETEAU

And commencing with France?

CAGLIOSTRO

With France, France marches in the avant-garde of nations. Let's put a torch in hand; the fire that it lights will illuminate the world.

RETEAU

But don't you fear?

CAGLIOSTRO

The tenderness of this people for its Queen, its love for its King?
You will see love and tenderness founder under our attacks
as quickly as this snow which is consecrated to them today.
And that's why the Grand Order has need of you, as perhaps
tomorrow it will have need of the locksmith who lodges in this
shop, or the minister who dwells in a palace. For the hour is
approaching and I intend that in five years we will be laughing
with pity as we tread underfoot the ruins of this Bastille.

(pointing to it with a gesture) On which our wives and daughters
will dance. And now, lead me into your dwelling, my brother, so
that you will know what the Grand Master expects of you.

(They leave.)

SAINT-LANDRY

(returning) That Portuguese must be Turkish—impossible to
soften him up.

THE PHILOSOPHER

And here the wind whips more sharply than yesterday!

SAINT-LANDRY

Where to find a ninny to pluck honestly or even dishonestly?

THE PHILOSOPHER

Alas—ninnies don't come out in such cold.

(shouts and noises off)

L'ARTAIGNE

Heavens! What's that shouting about?

THE PHILOSOPHER

A sleigh being assailed.

SAINT-LANDRY

They're throwing stones at it.

L'ARTAIGNE

It must have crushed some pedestrian.

SAINT-LANDRY

A cripple—competition.

POSITIVE

(going back) Down with the sledge.

SHOUTS

Down with cripples.

(Enter a sled harnessed to a very fine horse. On the bench are seated the Queen and Andrea. Weber, on the seat behind them, is driving trying to break through the crowd.)

POSITIVE

(shouting) To the Police!

SHOUTS

Yes, yes—to the Police.

THE PHILOSOPHER

But they are women.

SAINT-LANDRY

Women or men—if these were the ninnies we were searching for—

ANDREA

Ah! Madame, they are stopping the carriage.

QUEEN

Courage, Andrea! Courage.

PERINE

(to the crowd) Snowballs.

ALL

Snowballs.

(They riddle them with snowballs. The sleigh is in the middle of the stage.)

QUEEN

Weber—get us down.

(The lackey helps them down.)

PERINE

The horse is ours.

L'ARTAIGNE

Yes—ours!

SAINT-LANDRY

They will roast him on the brazier and eat him.

CROWD

Yes—yes—that's it.

(The crowd begins to break up the carriage.)

WOMAN

To eat food at last!

ANDREA

Madame—they're breaking up the sleigh.

QUEEN

Eh! Let them break it! Weber, do something about my horse, my brave Belus.

SAINT-LANDRY

There! Let's dismember the horse now.

CROWD

Hurrah!

(The Countess de la Motte is passing in a carriage, the commotion stops her. She puts her head out the carriage door.)

COUNTESS

I am not mistaken? Stop.

(she gets out of the carriage) Why, yes—it's indeed the Queen.

(she runs to the Queen and Andrea) You, Miladies, you here!

ANDREA

Ah, Countess, help us.

QUEEN

Especially help my poor Belus.

COUNTESS

(to Weber) Cut the harness—then jump in the saddle—make the animal rear on these cowards—and their ranks will open—then get going hell for leather.

(Weber edges into the crowd) As for us, let's observe—yes—there he is on horseback.

(Weber leaps on the horse which rears distributing kicks to the right and left—then rushing through the disarray. Shouts of Anger.)

ANDREA

Ah—there, he got out!

QUEEN

Ah, thanks, Countess.

COUNTESS

Now, let's think of ourselves.

PERINE

(to the crowd) It's the little one, the last who made him leave.

THE PHILOSOPHER

And who stole our supper from us.

L'ARTAIGNE

Now, they are laughing at us.

WOMAN

By Jove—girls from the Opera, dolls at the Soubise!

SAINT-LANDRY

They think they have the right to crush people because their lovers have wherewithal to pay the doctor—

L'ARTAIGNE

See the diamonds the little one has on her ears.

SAINT-LANDRY

Didn't I tell you! Here it is, the opportunity. Let's tear them from her!

THE PHILOSOPHER

Ears and all!

CROWD

Yes, yes.

SAINT-LANDRY

Death to crushers!

(They circle the women under the obelisk where the portraits of the king and queen are.)

QUEEN

They won't believe me. They are mad!

CROWD

Kill! Kill!

ANDREA

Ah, we are lost! And not one policeman.

COUNTESS

(escaping the cordon which encircles them) Ah!

(calling) Officer? Help—they are murdering women!

CHARNY

(sword in hand) Get back, bandits.

(he charges the assailants who recoil)

SAINT-LANDRY

Where did he come from?

THE PHILOSOPHER

Save yourself, if you can!

(Charny pursues them with blows from the tip and flat of the sword. They scatter. The coachman pursues them with blows of his whip.)

QUEEN

Ah! Sir, thanks with all my heart. You've saved us.

CHARNY

Miladies, it's for me in this situation to give you thanks with all my heart for having brought me a precious good fortune—to a courageous man!

QUEEN

Would you tell us your name, sir, so that we will at least know the name of our liberator?

CHARNY

Madame, it's not worth the trouble.

QUEEN

I beg you!

CHARNY

My name is Count Oliver de Charny.

ANDREA

My God! Now that our sleigh is broke, how are we going to get back?

COUNTESS

My carriage is at your disposition, Miladies! The carriage is shabby, war is war!

ANDREA

Two ladies alone with this man! At such an hour—

COUNTESS

You are right—it's not prudent. Wait.

QUEEN

(to Queen) What's she going to do?

COUNTESS

(To Charny, who is starting to leave) Mr. de Charny.

CHARNY

Madame?

COUNTESS

It seems to me that a gentleman like you wouldn't suffer himself to oblige us by half—am I mistaken?

CHARNY

Madame—dispose of me? What must I do?

COUNTESS

Simply climb up with these ladies in this carriage and accompany them.

CHARNY

Where to?

COUNTESS

To Versailles.

CHARNY

I am at the orders of these ladies and yours!

QUEEN

Once again thanks, Mr. de Charny.

(to Countess) But you, Countess.

COUNTESS

Oh! Me, I will find another carriage.

CHARNY

(looking to the right) Eh! Exactly, here's one.

COUNTESS

Thanks.

QUEEN

Ah! Countess—we owe you our life!

COUNTESS

(with a curtsy) Don't I owe mine to Your Majesty?

QUEEN

You recognized me? By what?

COUNTESS

By the portrait on this candy box that Your Majesty forgot at my place.

(she wants to give it to her)

QUEEN

You will bring it to me at Versailles, Countess, and I will prove to you that if you've long hoped for justice and protection—you will lose nothing by having waited for it.

(gaily) Come, Mr. de Charny—into the carriage!

(She prepares to get in the carriage, which has come up on the right. Charny gives her his hand up. He gets in and bows deeply to the Queen and Andrea.)

CAGLIOSTRO

(emerging from the left) Well, Mr. Gazetteer, it's agreed—I will soon furnish you a sensational article.

RETEAU

When it pleases you, Count.

CAGLIOSTRO

Why look there—I am not mistaken—it's really—

RETEAU

The Queen!

CAGLIOSTRO

In the streets of Paris at this hour. A man with two women and an officer.

RETEAU

(sneering) Her lover, no doubt? Here's the article we are seeking.

CAGLIOSTRO

Not at all. As spicy as this may be, mine will be even better.

CHARNY

(inside the coach) Hit it, coachman.

(The horse moves.)

QUEEN

(inside her coach) Till soon, Countess.

COUNTESS

(alone, after a curtsy) Come! I'll be late getting to the Cardinal's but I think he'll pardon me.

(She heads toward the boulevard while Cagliostro and Reteau point to her smiling while the robbers and beggars return from all sides, tossing snowballs at the carriage as it leaves.)

## CURTAIN

# ACT II

## SCENE 3: THE SHOP OF
## THE JEWELERS BOEHMER
## AND BOSSANGE

*Small jewelry shop, Qual d'École. In the back, a huge counter furnished with armchairs. Entry door to the left of this counter, decorated with an abundance of fancy locks and bolts. To the right, an armoire also furnished with huge locks. Another counter, much smaller in front of this armoire, perpendicular to the other—huge scales on the large counter. Small scales on the second.*

*At rise: Bossange is arranging jewels in a box. Boehmer enters from the right, glasses, glossy sleeves—feather pen in his ear—to the extent possible, Boehmer is tall and thin, Bossange is short and fat.*

BOSSANGE

(raising his hand) What is it my dear Boehmer?

BOEHMER

By Jove, it's a letter form the Financier Baudart de Saint-James, who demands payment of 500,000 pounds that he loaned us to finish this cursed necklace and urges us that since we cannot sell it in his arrangement to, to break it up to reimburse him.

BOSSANGE

Break up such a marvel! Profanation!

BOEHMER

My dear partner, you are an artist. As for me, I am a merchant, and a prodigy no one would call a nightingale in terms of commerce. You've seen that not one queen, not one court in Europe has been rich enough to pay for it. How can we be rich enough to keep it? No! No! Baudart is right, let's break it up— there's no other way to go anymore to avoid bankruptcy.

BOSSANGE

Boehmer, I beg you! Wait a little longer!

BOEHMER

Do you have a purchaser?

BOSSANGE

Well, yes, perhaps—

BOEHMER

Bah! And who is that?

BOSSANGE

The Queen.

BOEHMER

Her Majesty? She's refused it two times.

BOSSANGE

Listen, you know Laporte, our neighbor, the goldsmith. Well, for the last three months, he's had an excellent client, the Countess de la Motte-Valois, who is, it seems, in deep with the Cardinal de Rohan, but who is even better at court. The Queen sees only with her eyes. So Laporte, who is a good friend has thought to beg her to make Her Majesty reconsider this refusal which is ruining us. Why won't Madame LaMotte be as clever as the serpent?

BOEHMER

Because the apple which it is a question of making Eve pick, costs 1600 thousand pounds, my poor Bossange, and at that price, the serpent himself would have had his work cut out for him. Let's break it up, I tell you its the only way.

BOSSANGE

Wait—Laporte must have whispered to his client to come in passing to purchase some bauble from us. In the meantime, we will show her the necklace and try to put her in our interests. Make a trip to Baudart de Saint James and ask him for yet one more month—will you?

BOEHMER

(taking his hat) To oblige you! But I'm not confident.

(he leaves by the back)

BOSSANGE

(alone) Break up this admirable jewel—the 8th marvel of the world! And yet if this last safety anchor fails us, it will be necessary to reach that point. But who's coming?

DUCORNEAU

Pamphile Ducorneau, my dear Mr. Bossange, your little cousin after the fashion of Brittany.

BOSSANGE

(brutally) My cousin—you! Where'd you see that?

DUCORNEAU

Why on my birth certificate, since your great uncle Sulpice-Onesime Bossange married my great aunt Brigitte-Locadie Ducorneau.

BOSSANGE

Will you soon finish reciting your genealogical tree to me? I don't have the leisure to hear you.

DUCORNEAU

So much the worse—for I came to speak to you about your necklace for which I think I've found you a purchaser.

BOSSANGE

(abruptly changing manner) A buyer—sit down, my dear cousin and how is your worthy aunt?

DUCORNEAU

Not bad thanks. She died eleven years ago at Easter—but you now recognize me my rich cousin?

BOSSANGE

Pardon me. The weight of business—but you were saying you had found—

DUCORNEAU

Yes—you know that I have the honor of being Chancellor of the Ambassador of Portugal. Well, for four months the post has been vacant when abruptly, yesterday morning, an ambassador fell from heaven on us.

BOSSANGE

Ah!

DUCORNEAU

And what an ambassador! Once of the greatest Lords of Christianity, the Marques de Souza. Ah! You have to actually see him to know how noble he is! What Majesty! What elegance in his least gestures—they don't come any better!

BOSSANGE

Excuse me! But even such a great Lord as Mr de Souza may be I don't suppose that He would—

DUCORNEAU

Would wish to buy your treasure? No, it's Her Very Pious Majesty his sovereign.

BOSSANGE

The Queen of Portugal! The only one we didn't offer it to.

When will I have the honor of seeing your ambassador, my dear cousin?

DUCORNEAU

Why I am preceding him by only a few moments. And hold on, I believe I hear him—yes, he's getting out of his carriage with the First Secretary and his First Valet de Chamber.

BOSSANGE

(hurrying to the door) My cousin, my cousin, if the deal is made, your place will be set every Sunday. No, that's not enough, every Sunday and every Tuesday.

(The Portuguese is magnificently dressed, huge sash over shoulder. Beausire and Saint Landry are dressed as Secretary and First Valet. Opulent, tan complexions, very dark eyebrows with eccentric wigs.)

(Outside, with very pronounced Portuguese accent as are those of his acolytes)

THE PORTUGUESE

There—there! Give me your hand Iago and you the back, Ramírez. Oh! How rough this carriage is. Ah! It's you consul, Corno!

DUCORNEAU

(frowning, bent over) Myself, Milord.

THE PORTUGUESE

This here is the house of these jewelers?

DUCORNEAU

Yes, Milord, and I have the honor of presenting to Your Excellency, Mr. Bossange, one of the partners.

BOSSANGE

(eagerly) And the cousin of your Chancellor, Milord.

THE PORTUGUESE

That's fine, Íñigo.

BEAUSIRE

Milord—

THE PORTUGUESE

An armchair.

BOSSANGE

Here, Milord.

(pushes forward a chair)

BOSSANGE

Oh—forgive.

(pushes another one forward)

THE PORTUGUESE

Thanks—Ramírez.

SAINT-LANDRY

Milord.

THE PORTUGUESE

My tobacco.

SAINT-LANDRY

Here, Milord.

(He offers him a box from which the Portuguese takes tobacco, shaking the tobacco on his cuff like a great lord.)

DUCORNEAU

(to Bossange) Huh! What distinction!

THE PORTUGUESE

And tell me, Mr. Belauze?

BEAUSIRE

Bossange, Excellency.

THE PORTUGUESE

Right—Bossange—do you speak Portuguese?

BOSSANGE

Alas, no, Milord.

THE PORTUGUESE

(with a glance toward his acolytes) Ah! That's a shame. My Chancellor speaks it marvelously. All the same you have a national name, Cornone!

DUCORNEAU

Indeed—strictly—if Your Excellency wishes it.

THE PORTUGUESE

Yes, yes! But I won't keep you. It's the hour when your Chancellor opens—Especially pay, Mr. Cornone, pay with open bureaus— you have funds—?

DUCORNEAU

Oh! We have in the cash box nearly 110 thousand pounds.

BEAUSIRE and SAINT LANDRY

One hundred ten thousand.

THE PORTUGUESE

(severely) That's little—I told you, Íñigo, that we would be in need in Paris—go, Mr. Cornone, and if you need funds ask Íñigo for them.

(Ducorneau bows very low and leaves after a protective gesture from the Portuguese and Beausire.)

BEAUSIRE

Mr. Ducorneau has explained to you what it's all about?

BOSSANGE

Yes, Mr. Secretary and I am going to have the honor of presenting our necklace to the Ambassador.

(He offers a jewel box, after having opened it, to the Portuguese. After a moment, the latter rises, furious and tosses the box on the counter.)

THE PORTUGUESE

Íñigo, tell this merchant who shows to the Marquis de Souza some paste instead of diamonds, that I will complain to the minister and that I will send to the Bastille the comedian who tries to mystify an ambassador from Portugal! Come Ramírez!

(He head toward the door.)

BOSSANGE

I beg the Ambassador to deign to accept my excuses. But it is indeed permitted to take certain precautions when it's a question of a necklace which is a fortune in itself. We have so many thieves to worry about.

(The Portuguese still standing and very dignified exhales his rage in an incomprehensible gibberish that Beausire and Saint Landry accentuate with approving and respectful gestures of their heads.)

BEAUSIRE

(after the gibberish) His Excellency has charged me to tell you that he is annoyed that a jeweler to the crown of France is reduced to being unable to distinguish between an ambassador and a scoundrel. And His Excellency is withdrawing to his small hotel.

BOSSANGE

(hurriedly) Monsignor—Marquis—don't do that, Mr. Íñigo, Mr. Ramírez—I will be dishonored.

(The Portuguese resumes his gibberish but more conciliatory, shortly and ends by sitting down.)

BOSSANGE

Ah! Milord—such goodness!

(aside) Ooh! What trouble it is to sell!

(He opens the armoire at the right in which is a little armoire, from which he takes a jewel box that he opens with a thousand precautions).

BEAUSIRE

(low to the Portuguese, in his natural voice) Oof! What trouble there'll be to steal that!

BOSSANGE

Here!

(A pause. The Portuguese speaks in a low voice to Beausire and Saint Landry pointing to certain stones with his finger.)

BOSSANGE

Well?

BEAUSIRE

Well, the ambassador counts ten stones, lightly set!

BOSSANGE

His Excellency is difficult.

BEAUSIRE

Sir, in Brazil, Portuguese nobles play with diamonds the way children play with marbles!

BOSSANGE

Such as it is this necklace is the most beautiful matching of jewels there is in Europe.

THE PORTUGUESE

You are right, Mr. Grossange and it suits me. The price?

BOSSANGE

1600 thousand pounds, Monsignor.

THE PORTUGUESE

(1n a decided tone) 100 thousand pounds too dear!

BOSSANGE

Monsignor, to compose an ornament of this merit, there was necessary research, terrifying travel—if you knew them.

THE PORTUGUESE

(emphatic) 100 thousand pounds too dear!

BEAUSIRE

And it's necessary that a conviction once decided on by His Excellency, there's never any haggling.

THE PORTUGUESE

Never!

SAINT-LANDRY

Never!

BOSSANGE

Well, Monsignor, if despite the absence of my partner, I were to take upon myself to reach a lessening of the such importance, it is permitted of me to ask His Excellency what method of payment he will fix?

THE PORTUGUESE

100,000 pounds cash.

BOSSANGE

And the rest?

THE PORTUGUESE

In three payments stretched out from month to month in Lisbon. My first valet or my secretary will accompany you—

(with a meaningful tone) One is as good as the other.

BOSSANGE

Well, Monsignor, it's a deal agreed. Ah! Except for a slight reservation, and the Portuguese honor is delicate for His Excellency not to approve it.

THE PORTUGUESE

Indeed.

BOSSANGE

It's true our Queen has refused the necklace but it was made for her and we cannot allow it to leave France forever without asking Her Majesty if she hasn't changed her opinion.

THE PORTUGUESE

That's fair! And, gentlemen, I would expect that a Portuguese merchant would use the same language as Mr. Bossange.

BOSSANGE

Monsignor honors me! In a week I will have the honor of bringing a definitive answer to him at his hotel.

THE PORTUGUESE

That's fine. Come, Íñigo.

(he leaves supported by Beausire)

(Bossange confounds himself with bows.)

BEAUSIRE

(in his natural voice) The river has been turned.

SAINT-LANDRY

And the jeweler is on dry land.

BOSSANGE

(overwhelmed with joy) Sold! It's sold!

CURTAIN

# ACT II
## SCENE 4: THE DAIRY FARM
## OF THE PETIT TRIANON

*A section of the Queen's hamlet at the Petit Trianon at the right forming a portion of a circular arc, the Queen's house and the house called "Billard". In the rear, a lake shaded by trees. Between two of these trees a usable swing. To the left, the farm, the stable and the hen house. Flowers by the walls and windows. Tables and rustic chairs. The decor is sunny and gay.*

*At rise: The Marquis de Polastron is playing a violin sitting on a barrel, to the side seated on the grass, Mme de Campan and Baron de Besenval. The Princess Lamballe is seated on a bench, also the Count d'Adhemar and Andrea de Taverney. In the middle of the stage dancing to the rondau played by Polastron, the Queen, the Duchess de Polignac, the Countess de Challons, the Countess de Polastron, the Count d'Artois, the Count de Vaudreiul, the Duke de Coigny, the Duchess de Coigny. After a rondau is completed the Queen arrives, facing the audience and stops, the Queen sits by the dancers and the dance begins all over again. The women are in short white dresses and fantastic muslins.*

QUEEN

(sings) My daughter wants a bonnet (repeat)
Of fine chambray lace? (repeat)

No, no, no, mommie, no!
That's not my illness!
Gay! Gay! What a mother I've got.
Who doesn't hear her daughter's pain.
Gay! Gay! What a mother I have.
Who doesn't hear the pain I have!
My daughter wants a husband (repeat)
Who's good looking, who's well made? (repeat)
Oy, yoi, yoi, mommie, yes, you!
Now that's really my malady.
Gay! Gay! What a mother I've got.
Who doesn't hear her daughter's pain.
Gay! Gay! What a mother I have!
Who doesn't hear the pain I have!

ALL

(applauding) Bravo!

(A farm girl comes to speak a word to Mme Campan)

MME CAMPAN

(to Queen) Everything is prepared for your Majesty's pleasure.

QUEEN

Thanks, Campan, quick, Miladies, let's hurry for there's no Queen in the world who can prevent the cream from turning sour.

(Mme de Polignac, Mme de Challons, Mme de Polastron, run to the farm in front of which are placed large tables bearing pitchers of cream, strainers of cheese and bibs which they put over their dresses, helped by four servants.)

MME DE POLIGNAC

(hands in the cream) Vaudreuil, give me back my gloves.

(turns up her sleeves)

MME DE CHALLONS

Coigny, hitch my bib!

MME DE POLASTRON

Who wants to pour me my cream?

COUNT D'ARTOIS

I won't allow anyone that privilege.

COIGNY

(to Mme de Polignac) Decidedly the Count d'Artois is in good with Mme de Polastron.

MME DE POLIGNAC

With Bichette! Why certainly, it's only her husband who doesn't suspect it.

COIGNY

Bah! He has his violin to console him.

COUNT D'ARTOIS

By the way, Miladies, I have news to tell you.

MME DE CHALLONS

News! Speak up, Milord!

COUNT D'ARTOIS

You know that the crazy notoriety that Mr. Mesmer enjoys with the Parisians and especially the women, is becoming a furor.

MME DE POLASTRON

That's quite natural—he's so handsome!

COUNT D'ARTOIS

However much you may be his faithful acolytes, you Mme de Polignac, you Mme de Challons, you Mme de Polastron, the priestesses of fashion, it's a duty which you cannot escape. But guess who I discovered day before yesterday—the chain of the famous banquet enlaced around her body, eyes out of their orbits, head turned, arms, legs, feet beating wildly under the influence of fluid? I give you odds of 100-1000! or rather no—I bet you will guess—the most boring person in the Court.

ALL

Madame de Noailles.

COUNT D'ARTOIS

Touching unanimity! Yes, my sister, Madame de Noailles. Madame Etiquette convulsed, swooning—

(with horror) —and a low-cut gown.

ALL

Oh!

QUEEN

That must be terrifying.

COUNT D'ARTOIS

To a degree! So I took flight: I, who came to submit myself to the marvelous treatment of the doctor.

QUEEN

Oh! When you go back, my brother, take me—I'm dying to do it.

COUNT D'ARTOIS

With pleasure if the King permits—my sister, but despite Louis's—indulgence, I doubt he'll let you indulge this caprice.

QUEEN

Who knows? He actually let me play the Barber of Seville.

PRINCESS LAMBALLE

Is it possible? The King who told Mr. Beaumarchais—

COUNT D'ARTOIS

That if the Marriage of Figaro were ever played, the Bastille would have to be demolished.

MME DE POLASTRON

Still, Figaro had a full hall.

MME DE POLIGNAC

And the Bastille is still standing.

QUEEN

Ah! My God! And here I am forgetting my chickens—it's time for their lunch. Andrea, take my place for a minute or my cheese will be missing. My brother, my seeds.

(The Count turns the box over in her apron and she opens the henhouse door calling!)

QUEEN

Chicks! Chicks!

(She throws them seeds, the hens come to eat them.)

MME DE CHALLONS

Mme Coigny, a swing, if you please?

COUNT D'ARTOIS

(in a low voice seated at the table) Say, sis—is it true what they're saying?

QUEEN

What's that?

COUNT D'ARTOIS

That the credit of the Duchess de Polignac is low and that Your Majesty now has the Countess de la Motte-Valois for favorite. There, see Miss de Taverney, your other great friend—she seems quite sad.

QUEEN

What childishness—am I forbidden to make a pleasant face to someone who pleases!

(she tosses the last handful of grain to the chicken coop and the chickens go back in) There—see, the meal's over.

MME DE LAMBALLE

My turn, Mr. de Coigny.

QUEEN

Yet it's true, Andrea, that you are sad?

ANDREA

(with a manner of confession) Me, sad! Your Majesty is mistaken!

QUEEN

No, and it's not today. Oh! I've actually noticed when this took you—hold on, it's sometime after our famous adventure at the Port Saint Martin. You are blushing—fie! How bad it is to be jealous, Andrea.

ANDREA

Me, jealous, Madame! And of whom?

QUEEN

Why of the Countess de la Motte-Valois, since it's from that day that I began to show friendship to her.

ANDREA

I swear to Your Majesty that you are mistaken. I am not jealous—be certain of it!

QUEEN

And you are right, Andrea, for my heart is large enough for all those that I love. But by the way, that officer who behaved so gallantly with us—have you seen him since?

ANDREA

Never, Madame.

QUEEN

He seemed charming to me, didn't you like him, Andrea?

ANDREA

Madame, that night was so dark that I was barely able to see him.

COUNT D'ARTOIS

Sister, these ladies are demanding a game of blind man's buff.

Are you in it?

QUEEN

Willingly. Here's my cheese finished.

(she tastes it) And it is delicious!

MME DE CHALLONS

Let fate decide—Count, sir.

(each bustles around him)

COUNT D'ARTOIS

Oh! Ladies.

(making them in a circle) One, two, three.

(like a child) I'll go into the trees—four, five, six—to pick cherries—seven, eight, nine, in my hamper—ten, eleven, twelve, they'll all be red.

QUEEN

(happily) It's me! It's me!

COUNT D'ARTOIS

No cheating, sis.

(they put a blindfold on her eyes)

MME DE POLIGNAC

How many fingers?

QUEEN

Twelve.

(Game of blind man's buff, the Queen tries to catch those present, they avoid her.)

MME DE POLIGNAC

Danger!

(The King enters in the middle of the game.)

QUEEN

Ah! I've caught someone.

COUNT D'ARTOIS

Who is it?

QUEEN

Wait.

(placing her hands over the shoulder and the face of the King) It's the King!

COUNT D'ARTOIS

She's won.

KING

Excuse me for coming to disturb your games, Madame. I had a
favor to ask of you.

QUEEN

And, me, too. But first of all, how can I be agreeable to Your
Majesty?

KING

Madame, at Trianon, you are at home and you receive only
your friends. Would you permit me today to bring to you one of
mine? The Bailiff of Suffren.

ALL

Oh!

QUEEN

Mr. the Bailiff de Suffren has just given seven great battles
without enduring one defeat. And at the very time he is the
friend of the King, he is the honor of France. I won't receive
him with pleasure but with joy.

KING

Madame, I thank you. My dear Calonne, would you inform the
nephew of the Bailey, who accompanied us here, so that the
Queen can address her invitation to him herself.

(Calonne leaves bowing) By the way, Madame, you had something to request from me—what's it all about?

QUEEN

(on the side) Of letting me go to Paris, once, Sire!

KING

To Paris! Where?

QUEEN

Place Vendome—to Mr. Mesmer's.

KING

The devil! Still, a day where you grant me a favor, I cannot refuse a whim to you. I place only one condition on it, it's that you become accompanied by Mme de Lamballe and Miss de Taverney—in that manner I will be at ease. Is it agreed?

QUEEN

Agreed, sire.

KING

(kissing by hand) Then I sign—but here's the young officer we were waiting for. Madame, I present you the Count de Charny.

QUEEN

(aside) Him!

ANDREA

(aside) Him!

KING

Who's covered himself with glory in America with Mr de Lafayette and has just continued that tradition with Mr. the Bailiff de Suffren. He will retell to his commander the favor with which you wish to honor him.

(Charny has bowed respectfully to the Queen, then the King and starts to withdraw.)

KING

Hold on, Mr. de Charny. I have still something to tell you in front of the Queen. Imagine, Madame, that in this last battle given by Mr. de Suffren to the English, the Captain of the Severe, one of my ships had handed down his colors, when the lieutenant of the ship, who was watching the batteries, noticing that the firing ceased, leapt on the bridge and saw suddenly the colors lowered and the Captain about to surrender. At this sight, all the French blood in his veins revolted. He seized the flags at the same time ordering fire to recommence—then nailed it beneath the pennant.

ALL

Ah!

KING

It's by this means that the Severe was kept for me.

QUEEN

Fine action.

COUNT D'ARTOIS

Brave Action.

KING

Come close, Mr. de Charny.

CHARNY

(very simple) Madame, what I did ten of my comrades would have thought to have done at the same time as me. I executed it first, that's all. The captain of the Severe was a brave officer who, for a moment, lost his head. Our determination gave him the respite he required, and, from that moment, he was the bravest of us all. That's why I beg Your Majesty not to exaggerate the merit of my action! That would crush this poor officer who cries every day for a moment's forgetfulness.

QUEEN

Mr. de Charny, you are an honest man

(with a nuance of meaning) It suffices to see you a single time to be sure of it. I think that you will do me the pleasure of accompanying the Bailiff here.

(she extends her hand, Charny kisses it) By the way, Sire, since I am keeping Your Majesty, I will take you to see my new buildings. Come, Miladies, let those who are not worn out come do the King the honors of our village. Till soon, Mr. de Charny.

ANDREA

Mr. de Charny, I have great pleasure in seeing you again for I am indebted to you and I will never forget it. In such a brilliant court as this my only support is the kindness which Her Majesty deigns to show me. But I don't even have that weak credit to offer you, since on that side you are, you see, more greatly favored than I.

CHARNY

Indeed, Miss, you can do much for me and since you have the luck to be one of those Her Majesty loves, I beg you to intercede with her—to—

ANDREA

To obtain advancement for you? A regiment, perhaps?

CHARNY

For me to leave France as soon as possible. Mr. de Suffren won't go back to sea for a few months. I want to leave before that. The fighting has started again in America. Let me be allowed to return.

ANDREA

Leave! But only to run new dangers—you must have no one who loves you in that case.

CHARNY

No one!

ANDREA

And to distance yourself when you can count on Her Majesty's favor you must have a grave reason.

CHARNY

Yes—an imperious motive commands me, directs me to flee. Ah! God! If you knew, if you could know—

ANDREA

What then?

CHARNY

(trying to get hold of himself) Nothing—nothing Miss—Excuse me.

ANDREA

Mr. de Charny, I don't wish to force your secrets. The privilege of having deserved the Queen's confidence should not constrain you from granting me yours.

CHARNY

(very upset) Ah! Miss—if I could speak, you would be the first to whom I would open my heart.

(vehemently after controlling himself) And yet, no! No! To you less than to all others have I the right to betray what I am suffering.

ANDREA

(aside) To me less than all others?

CHARNY

For I am suffering—Ah! cruelly—and that since the first day I saw you—with the Queen!

(gesture by Andrea) And that's why I must leave!

ANDREA

From the first day he saw me.

(seeing the Queen) The Queen.

ANDREA

Madame, here's Mr. de Charny who hardly returned to Versailles, wants to ask you to leave us to go to America so as to fight again! But I think to answer to the wishes of the Queen, by praying her, on the contrary, to keep our defender with us.

CHARNY

Ah! Miss—this is treachery.

QUEEN

Miss de Taverney's right, Mr. de Charny. Your worth is already too precious to us for us to renounce you in favor of Mr. Washington.

CHARNY

(bowing) I am the very devoted servant of the Queen.

ANDREA

Are you mad at me for it, Mr. de Charny?

CHARNY

Oh! Miss, how could you think so!

ANDREA

(aside, leaving) Could his illness be the same as mine?

QUEEN

Mr. de Charny, I have a question to put to you; why weren't you more surprised just now when the King presented you to me, in finding your companion of the carriage?

CHARNY

Because on the morning of this day to which the Queen alludes, I found myself face to face with her carriage when she was coming to visit the Place Bourbon, to the Duchess de Polignac.

QUEEN

Then you knew who I was—for the last four months?

CHARNY

Yes, Madame.

QUEEN

And for the last four months you haven't tried to remind me of the service you rendered me?

CHARNY

It's hardly as though I even recalled that the Queen had deigned to call on me.

(pause) Your Majesty seems astonished at my response.

QUEEN

It's because I think that all men of this Court who for a word less indifferent than is customary would not have hesitated to publicly compromise the Queen of France. Coigny for a flower, Vaudreuil for a handkerchief, Lauzan for a minute, Fersen for a smile, what would they have said, these seducers, if chance had cast them during half the night on the cushions of a carriage with the Queen dozing almost in their arms? But, perhaps you forgot that, like the rest of it?

CHARNY

(mastering a violent emotion) Yes, Madame, I'd forgotten it.

QUEEN

Luckily, Mr. de Charny, my memory is not as short as yours. But time is passing and you must deliver the King's message to Mr. de Suffren—till later.

(Charny bows deeply and leaves) Yes, that one is truly a gentleman! Alas! How many remain so today?

(seeing Mme de la Motte enter) At last, Countess—you are here.

COUNTESS de la MOTTE

May Your Majesty excuse me but I was returning for her service.

QUEEN

For my service?

COUNTESS de la MOTTE

The Queen will deign to grant a moment's audience to her jeweler who's coming to accomplish a duty to her.

QUEEN

A duty?

COUNTESS de la MOTTE

(who's made a sign to Bossange) It's about that beautiful diamond necklace, Your Majesty didn't want to accept.

QUEEN

The necklace.

(laughing) We're back to that! Ah, the fact is that it is beautiful, Mr. Bossange! What consoles me is that it cost a million and a half, so much that I was unable—that if I couldn't buy it no one will have it.

BOSSANGE

Now that's what the duty is that I am coming to fulfill to Her Majesty. The necklace is sold.

QUEEN

(surprised and annoyed) Sold! To whom?

BOSSANGE

To Her Majesty, the Queen of Portugal!

QUEEN

(after a moment's hesitation) Well, so much the better for the Queen of Portugal. And let's not talk of it anymore.

BOSSANGE

To the contrary, may Your Majesty permit me to speak of it—for the purchase must go through only in the case that the Queen doesn't reverse her decision and I've brought the necklace so she can see it one last time.

QUEEN

No, no. Look, Countess, you're a woman, this will amuse you.

COUNTESS de la MOTTE

Admirable! Admirable! Ah! Mr. Bossange is right; there's only one Queen worthy of wearing this necklace, it's Your Majesty.

QUEEN

What are you doing, Countess?

COUNTESS de la MOTTE

(taking a mirror that Bossange passes to her) Oh! Your Majesty is sublime like this.

QUEEN

(looking in the mirror for a moment) Yes—they are superb jewels! Alas.

COUNTESS de la MOTTE

This necklace has touched Your Majesty. It is sacred and now ought not to be worn by anyone. Go now, Mr. Bossange— tomorrow the Queen will tell you if she will keep it—yes or no.

(Bossange bows and leaves.)

QUEEN

Countess, Countess, you are mad.

COUNTESS de la MOTTE

No, for I have a confession to make, Your Majesty.

QUEEN

A confession—what is it?

COUNTESS de la MOTTE

Since the Queen has deigned to cover me with kindness, I have not hidden from her that several times favors had obliged me to Cardinal de Rohan.

QUEEN

I don't know—I didn't remember—no matter, speak.

COUNTESS de la MOTTE

Well, this very morning the Cardinal did me the honor of paying me a visit for a charity that I preside over and as he asked me if the Queen would not take an interest in the unfortunate I committed the indiscretion of expressing to him the inexhaustible generosity which makes Her Majesty slave to her own kindness. I said that if the Queen had been less prodigal with me and with others, she would certainly have had in her cash box wherewithal to give herself this beautiful necklace so nobly, so courageously, but allow me to say it, so unjustly rejected. Ah! Madame! If you had seen, in learning of your heroic sacrifice, if you had seen Mr. de Rohan go pale!

QUEEN

(ironic) Go pale! Him?

COUNTESS de la MOTTE

It's not for me to defend someone who has been unfortunate enough to fall into disgrace with Her Majesty. He is really guilty since he has displeased the Queen.

QUEEN

Mr. de Rohan didn't displease me, he offended me. But I am Queen and Christian and doubly born, consequently, to forget offenses.

COUNTESS de la MOTTE

Ah! Madame! in that case, I'm sure of it, you will pardon Mr. de Rohan when you learn what he has done.

QUEEN

In that case, what did he do, countess?

COUNTESS de la MOTTE

Hardly had Mr. de Rohan learned that the Portuguese had purchased these jewels, "It's no longer a question of pleasure," he shouted, "but the royal dignity. I know the mind of these foreign courts, they will laugh at the Queen of France who has not enough money to satisfy a legitimate taste. No! Never!" He left me abruptly and went to the jewelers, where, during the absence of Mr. de Bossange, who is still unaware of the act—he purchased the diamonds from his partner.

QUEEN

Purchased the diamonds—1,500 thousand pounds—and what was his intention in this madness?

COUNTESS de la MOTTE

That since they could not be Your Majesty's they at least wouldn't be another woman's.

QUEEN

And you are sure that it isn't to make a gift of it to some mistress that de Rohan purchased this necklace?

COUNTESS de la MOTTE

I am sure that it's to destroy them rather than see them shine on the neck other than the Queen's.

QUEEN

(after a slight pause) What Mr. de Rohan did there, he did with a noble heart and from a delicate devotion. You will thank him for me, Countess. You will add that his friendship toward me is henceforth proven and that as for me, as an honest man as my Cousin Catherine says, accept the friendship on the condition of revenge. Also, I do not accept the gift from Mr. de Rohan.

COUNTESS de la MOTTE

What then, Madame?

QUEEN

Why his advancement! The King recently gave me the pension of 250 thousand pounds which he gives me each month.

(she pulls out her billfold) And as Mr. de Calonne has told me today, that if I need money his coffers are at my discretion. I could in a few days reimburse a portion of my debt to His Eminence. I will dispose of the surplus from month to month. In this manner, I will have this necklace which pleases me so much, and if I am troubled paying for it, at least I won't be troubling the King. I have earned moreover, by learning that I have a delicate friend, and a friend who has understood me.

(she offers her hand to the Countess)

COUNTESS de la MOTTE

(kissing it) Ah! Madame!

QUEEN

Countess, you will inform Mr. de Rohan that he will soon be

welcome at Versailles and that I have compliments to pay him.

(she leaves)

COUNTESS de la MOTTE

Come! I think I've managed the business of my ally well. And I will decidedly take the place of Madame de Prie without too much damage to France.

(seeing Cagliostro) Mr. Cagliostro!

CAGLIOSTRO

Myself, Countess.

COUNTESS de la MOTTE

By what miracle at the Trianon?

CAGLIOSTRO

Because I had the luck to offer to Antoine Richard the gardener of this residence, a Robinia grandeflora which gave joy to His Majesty and envy to Mr. Jassien, I have my formal and informal entrances here. I am profiting by it to stroll about, you know how I love to stroll in life.

COUNTESS de la MOTTE

You stroll—and you observe.

CAGLIOSTRO

You said it. Thus, I observe, Countess you have a joyful air.

COUNTESS de la MOTTE

Joy that you will share. You who are the friend of the Cardinal and who know like me what his ambition is.

CAGLIOSTRO

To return to the graces of an illustrious Princess who holds rancor against him because of certain reports that used to be sent from Vienna. Were you able, Countess, to dissipate these prejudices?

COUNTESS de la MOTTE

Her Majesty just ordered me to tell her Grand Almoner that he would be very welcome near her. And that the disfavor of the Queen was the only obstacle which stood between His Eminence and a ministerial portfolio—you will conclude from that, as I do that—

CAGLIOSTRO

That our Prime Minister, this poor Mr. de Breteuil, is indeed ill. And you are speaking to me of miracles! But what shall I say of yours? Yes, surely His Eminence must be indeed lucky, for if your ingenious friendship has succeeded in preparing this dazzling revenge for his vanity it may yet triumph further by—

COUNTESS de la MOTTE

What?

CAGLIOSTRO

Why—his love, Countess.

COUNTESS de la MOTTE

His love—for whom?

CAGLIOSTRO

Oh! Countess, as if you didn't know better than anyone, the devouring passion which for so long has distractedly absorbed the most gallant of prelates! As if he could hold back before so faithful a partner the burning tears which have poured out ten times before his familiar over the blonde tresses paid in one night of folly, he paid 100 crowns for—to the Queen's hair-dresser!

COUNTESS de la MOTTE

(aside, very upset) Of the Queen—he loves the Queen—

(aloud) Excuse me, isn't it natural that not knowing this secret known to the whole world.

CAGLIOSTRO

To the contrary, Countess, and your reserve proves once more your diplomatic finesse. But I am running on—and I'm forgetting that I have a meeting in Paris. Yes, a business meeting—with a person who is not a stranger to you, I believe—Mr. Reteau de Villette.

COUNTESS de la MOTTE

Indeed!

CAGLIOSTRO

An acquaintance of bad times.

(kissing her hand) Ah! Countess, how distant they are!

(aside, leaving) Come! I've sewn the seed, the land is fertile, it will germinate!

(He leaves.)

COUNTESS de la MOTTE

(alone) I'm choking—I thought I was going to faint. He no longer loves me! Come on! As if he had ever loved me! He used me, that's all! A caprice will carry away what a caprice brought, and he'll dismiss me like one of the opera girls who preceded me in his heart with a few jewels or a bundle of bills of exchange. And he spoke to me of sharing power! Of being two to reign! As if once his mistress, she would allow another woman to be beside him. She, the Austrian! And I loved this traitor! I, whose heart never beat for anyone! Oh, I intend to avenge myself—to avenge myself cruelly! On him and on her who stole him from me! Ah! They intend to cast me back into the mud from which I came! Well, I won't fall into it alone!

(Enter the Queen and her ladies and some gentlemen.)

QUEEN

(low to Countess) I've seen Mr. de Calonne, Countess, and he told me that we can count on 500 thousand pounds at the end of this month.

MR. DE CRUSSOL

The King, Madame.

(Louis XVI enters with Bertreuil, Calonne, Charny, de Suffren.)

KING

(to Queen) Madame, I'm bringing to you, the Bailiff de Suffren, the conqueror of Tringuemale and Gondelour, the terror of our English neighbors. He's my John Bart!

QUEEN

Sir, I don't have praise to give you, simply know that you haven't given a single battle for the glory of France without my heart beating in gratitude for you.

SUFFREN

It's the entire army, Madame, all these valiant sailors who are my children on whom such a flattering greeting as Your Majesty deigns to make me, reflects.

KING

By the way, Madame, with the money that I wanted to use to purchase those diamonds that you so nobly refused,

(The Queen and the Countess start.)

KING

I am going to construct a ship that I was going to call in memory of your virtue, "The Queen's Necklace.) Would you permit me to give it another name?

QUEEN

Yes, Sire—we will call it the Suffren and I will be the godmother of it with the Bailiff.

KING

You've guessed my idea—as always! Come, gentlemen, long
live Suffren!

ALL

(with enthusiasm) Long live Suffren!

(The Bailiff kisses the hands of the Queen.)

**CURTAIN**

# ACT II
## SCENE 5: THE WORKSHOP OF LOUIS XVI'S LOCKSMITH

*Door with a window giving on the Park of Versailles, two side doors.*

GAMAIN

(to the King, who is working on a lock) Then, it doesn't work.

KING

(in shirt sleeves, polishing and laboring at his bench) No, Gamain—it's useless for me to work on this satanic lock—the mug of the key actually tears the large beard, the large beard describes indeed the better half of the circle, but reaching there, it doesn't escape.

GAMAIN

(importantly) Let's see it! By Jove—it's because the shoulder is very small. I don't understand why you didn't see it. Since we've worked together, Your Majesty must have been thinking of a bunch of stupid things. I bet you were again deceived in politics.

KING

Damn! Gamain—that's a bit my role.

GAMAIN

Ah! You are very mistaken. You would do much better to not bother yourself with locksmithing.

KING

Ah! I would do better—but make me see—

GAMAIN

Like this! As soon as the key has released the large beard, it has to be able to open the bolt that it's just locked, and for that to engage the second beard, right?

KING

Yes—yes—

GAMAIN

(chaffing) Yes, yes—Well! How do you expect it will catch if the internal is not equal to the thickness of the muzzle?—more than a bit of freedom. No use for you to be King of France—vain to say "I want it" the little key says, "I don't want it" and good night—here, it's as if you were squabbling with your wife—she's always the stronger.

KING

I understand.

GAMAIN

(drinking) Sir, you've got a royal chamberlain there.

KING

To your health, Gamain.

GAMAIN

To yours, Sire, and to that of your lady. I mean to say the Queen, although—

KING

Although—finish, Gamain. Is it that my people are not content with their sovereign?

GAMAIN

Oh! Sire—we don't forget the kindnesses of the Queen for the poor, in the past winter. But damn! The Polignac costs her a great deal, and us, too. They say at my café—the Café of the Social Contract—that the Duchess Jules costs France twenty millions, and hell! Twenty millions is a lot for one duchess and even for two.

KING

They exaggerate at your café, Gamain—a sovereign must pay her servants. Don't you pay your apprentices?

GAMAIN

Yes, but not as expensively as that. Come on, good! Here's someone coming to bother us—always your ministers with their foolishness.

KING

No—it's the Count of Provence.

COUNT

Hello brother, greetings, Master Gamain—am I bothering you?

KING

No, my lesson is finished. Come on, till Tuesday next, Gamain—wait, here's something to purchase toys for your children.

GAMAIN

(who's put his vest back on) Many thanks, Sire—and a great deal of pleasure, Milord.

(to the King) Especially, may Your Majesty not get too rusty between now and Tuesday.

(He leaves.)

KING

You have something to tell me, my brother?

COUNT

My word no, I entered in passing, quite simply—ah, but still! But there's no need to weary Your Majesty with—

KING

What's it all about?

COUNT

Another pamphlet, Sire—against the Queen precisely—I have it on me—"The Fits of the Princess Etteniotna at the Fakir Remsem's"—switch the letters—Etteniotna, that's Antoinette and Remsem—

KING

(reading over the Count's shoulder) It's Mesmer—thanks, brother—

COUNT

Look, Sire, the description of the fit of the Princess Etteniotna, her contortions, her voluptuous disorder.

KING

(snatching the book) Infamy!

(De Breteuil, Calonne enter.)

KING

Before speaking of anything else, Breteuil, who is this by—?

BRETEUIL

Etteniotna—by a publisher named Reteau, Sire.

KING

He's in the Bastille, I suppose?

BRETEUIL

Sire, I have the order of imprisonment all prepared but before having it executed, I thought perhaps it would be better to give this wretch a bag of money and send him to go get himself hanged elsewhere.

KING

Why?

BRETEUIL

Because, Sire, when these wise guys tell a lie, the public is quite at ease to see them whipped, even hanged, but if unluckily, they are putting their hand on the truth.

KING

The truth?

BRETEUIL

Sire, saving the respect that I owe Your Majesty, a Queen of France who ventures in the midst of this equivocal world, and who goes there alone—

KING

Alone! You are mistaken Mr. de Breteuil, I indeed permitted the Queen to go to the tub of Mesmer—but I enjoined her to take with her a reliable person—irreproachable, even saintly.

BRETEUIL

Oh! Would it had been that way! If a woman like Mme de Lamballe, for example.

KING

It was exactly the Princess de Lamballe or in default of her, Miss de Taverney that I designated.

COUNT

Unfortunately, neither the one nor the other accompanied her—

KING

(to Crussol, who enters) Mr. Crussol—beg Madame de Lambelle or Miss de Taverney to come here immediately.

CRUSSOL

Sire, Ms. de Taverney is strolling right now in the park with the Queen and Mme la Motte-Valois.

KING

(to his brother) If the disobedience was as you say, sir—I must punish and I will punish.

ANDREA

(curtsying) What does Your Majesty wish of me?

KING

Information, Miss—what day did you to go Mr. Messmer's

home—in the company of the Queen?

ANDREA

Last Thursday, Sire—that is to say around four.

COUNT

Pardon me, Miss—but you were with the Queen?

ANDREA

Yes, Milord, with the Queen as the King, I think, had autho-
rized.

KING

(with relief) Indeed! Ah! Now I can breathe for Ms. de Taverney
never lies.

ANDREA

Never, Sire.

BRETEUIL

Oh! Never! But then, Sire, allow me—

KING

Yes—yes, I permit, you Breteuil, I am placing Ms. de Taverney
on the culprit's stool. Question her!

ANDREA

(smiling) Still, Sire, torture is abolished.

KING

Yes, I abolished it for others, but it hasn't been abolished for me.

BRETEUIL

First of all, Ms. de Taverney, can you tell me what the Queen was wearing?

ANDREA

Her Majesty wore a pearl gray taffeta, a braided muslin mantle, and a red velour cap—with big black ribbons.

KING

Is this the description of your agents?

BRETEUIL

No, Sire.

KING

(rubbing his hands) And what did the Queen do on entering?

ANDREA

Sire, Your Majesty is right to say "on entering" hardly had we put a foot on the first salon when a woman approached Her Majesty begging her not to go farther.

COUNT

(vexed) This is extraordinary!

KING

One moment! Do you know who this woman was that stopped her?

ANDREA

Yes, Sire, it was the Countess de la Motte-Valois.

KING

That intriguer.

COUNT

That beggar—she must be interrogated.

KING

No—the Queen is so good that the pretext of misery leads her to wherever there are equivocal folks in the nobility. I prefer to deprive myself of the immense relief that the complete absolution of the Queen would give me rather than see her facing that creature.

QUEEN

(who entered a moment before) And yet you will see her, Sire.

(she gestures to the Countess who is behind her to enter) Madame, would you please, I beg you, tell His Majesty what you did the day of my visit to Mr. Mesmer's—no reticence, no circumspection—only the truth!

COUNTESS

(aside) Have I got my vengeance? Oh! No! It's not enough for what I've suffered.

KING

Well, Madame, do you remember?

COUNTESS

Sire, I went to Mr. Mesmer's from curiosity like all Paris goes there. The spectacle seemed gross to me. I was returning when suddenly in the doorway I noticed Her Majesty with Miss de la Taverney. When I saw her august features, it seemed to me that the presence of the Queen was perhaps improper in this place. It was a flash of woman's instinct. I humbly ask pardon of Her Majesty if I overstepped the bounds of respect that I owe her.

QUEEN

Well, Sire, have you heard?

KING

I have no need of Madame's testimony. When the Queen says something she has no need to get witnesses to verify her speech. When the Queen has my approval she has nothing to seek from anyone and she has my approval.

QUEEN

And I thank Your Majesty for it.

COUNT

(hypocritically) Believe me, sister, that no one is as happy as I am to see you crush slander yet again.

QUEEN

I think I'll often give you that joy because slander never tires, as you know, better than anyone, my dear brother.

CALONNE

(in a low voice) I am going immediately to get Her Majesty to sign the credit the Queen has asked me for.

QUEEN

(in a low voice) Thanks.

(Exit the Queen and the ladies.)

KING

Now, gentlemen, let's get to work! What's new, Breteuil?

BRETEUIL

No great thing, Sire—just this loan project for the next year that Your Majesty approved in the last Council meeting.

KING

(sighing) Always borrowing, without knowing how to repay—that's still a problem.

BRETEUIL

Sire, a loan, it's the outpouring of a spring—the water vanishes here to spring up abundantly later—

KING

So be it—here's your signatures! Yours, Calonne.

CALONNE

(gaily) Now that we have money, Sire, let's spend it.

KING

(looking at the list) Ah! Ah! Right! The list is not long.

(looking at the total) What, a million one hundred thousand pounds total—for so few items?

CALONNE

Your Majesty noticed one of those items alone costs 500 thousand pounds.

KING

Which—Mr. Controller General?

CALONNE

The advance made to Her Majesty, the Queen, Sire.

KING

Five hundred thousand pounds to the Queen? That's not

possible—I gave her her pension myself five days ago.

CALONNE

Sire, if the Queen lacks money—you know how Her Majesty uses it—it's not extraordinary.

KING

No, no, if the Queen lacks money, she will have only more merit by waiting, and as for me, I guarantee you she will wait.

CALONNE

Sire, the Queen never asks unless forced by necessity.

KING

The needs of the Queen are less imperious than those of the poor—matter understood!

CALONNE

Then you cancel this credit, Sir?

KING

Yes, surely—and it seems to me I hear from here the generous voice of the Queen thanking me for having understood her heart so well. Now, that's her voice coming back—you are going to see.

(opening the window door) You are going for a stroll, Madame?

QUEEN

Yes, Sire, and are you doing good work?

KING

Judge! I've earned you 500,000 pounds.

QUEEN

(low to Countess) He has signed.

KING

Imagine that Mr. de Calonne was bringing you—on credit—a half million.

QUEEN

Oh!

KING

Yes, and then as for me, I scratched it out. There's 500,000 pounds saved.

QUEEN

What do you mean—scratched it out?

KING

Quite simply, this is going to do you an enormous good. They will applaud you the first time that you go to the Opera.

(showing the lock he's made) It works, see—the key engages the second link now that the internal is equal to the thickness of the muzzle—not a bit of liberty. You understand?

BRETEUIL

Yes, yes, Sir!

CALONNE

(low to the Queen) Ah, Madame, I am desolated.

KING

Good evening, Madame, I'm very hungry. And truly I've earned my supper.

(leaving, aside) Come, Gamain and the Café of the Social Contract will be pleased with me. Come, gentlemen.

COUNTESS

He struck it out!

MME DE POLIGNAC

And there are those who say we ruin the finances.

QUEEN

(to Madame de Polignac) Duchess, go find me a large box of red morocco which is in my violet armoire. Hurry! Hurry!

(Mme de Polignac leaves.)

QUEEN

Ah! Countess, this will punish me for being coquettish and hiding things from the King. All that was needed was this check to prove to me how much trouble I'm going to expose myself to. Let's go simply, why let's go honestly.

MME DE POLIGNAC

(returning) Here's what Her Majesty asked of me.

QUEEN

Thanks, Duchess.

(to Mme de Polignac) You are going to return the box to Boehmer & Bossange, Countess.

COUNTESS

Return it? But Your Majesty gave him 200,000 pounds deposit.

QUEEN

I abandon them on the condition the sale is off. The jeweler, gentlemen, shall not complain. Take it, Countess, take it.

COUNTESS

But Madame, why not ask for a delay?

QUEEN

To ask is to humiliate oneself! I understand humiliating oneself to save a living creature, were it one's dog, but to have the right to keep these stones—no way! Take it! Countess—only request for a receipt from the jewelers and thank Mr. de Rohan for his good grace and good will. Ah—having taken this decision, I feel much lighter.

(She leaves.)

COUNTESS

(alone) Well now! I asked from my revenge—I have it!

**CURTAIN**

# ACT II
## SCENE 6: THE GARDEN OF
## THE PALACE-ROYAL

*A corner of the garden of the Palace Royal. To the left, the Café Foy, whose tables extend to a book shop in a sort of kiosk. At the back, newly built galleries. To the right, thick arbors of elms hewn into a portico.*

*Strollers that represent the celebrated engraving of Debucourt.*

A MERCHANT OF COCOA

Refreshments, who wants to drink?

A MERCHANT OF RAT POISON

Death to Rats! Merchant of Rat Poison.

A SHOPKEEPER

Flowers—ladies, gentlemen.

YOUNG MAN IN BLACK

No, I already told you just now.

(to lady selling newspapers) Do you have my Paris newspaper?

Miss Nicolette?

NICOLETTE

Here it is.

YOUNG MAN IN BLACK

And say, do you also have that new brochure about which there's so much talk?

NICOLETTE

Etteniotna?

MARAT

At the Fakir Remsen's?

NICOLETTE

I think so. I sold the ten copies they left me. I'm going to be forced to send to the printer for it.

MARAT

(with an ironic smile) The Parisians love their Queen so much that all that's said about her interests them. Bye, Miss Nicolette.

NICOLETTE

Goodbye Mr. Marat.

(Marat distances himself.)

MERCHANT OF RAT POISON

Death to Rats!

COCOA MERCHANT

Refreshments

LOTTERY CRIER

(to the hunchback) Ask here for the list of numbers from the royal lottery.

PHILOMENE

(and other women touch the hump of the crier) Oh! Good luck! Good luck!

A BOURGEOIS

(to Philomene) Plague! Pretty eyes—where do you live, my beautiful child?

PHILOMENE

Where do you live, my handsome gentleman?

ZEPHYR

Heavens, Corisandra, what are you doing there?

CORISANDRA

Me, I'm waiting for someone—but I don't know who.

SHOPKEEPER

Flowers, ladies?

NINA

(to Amarinthe, seeing two Englishmen enter) Attention! Some Milords! It's Providence at the Palais-Royal.

AMARINTHE

Oh, what a misfortune not to know English.

NINA

But as for me, walking before the Englishmen with engaging airs—(pronouncing clumsily)—Regent Street—Westminster.

AMARINTHE

Westminster—Regent Street.

AN ENGLISHMAN

Yah! English.

(The Englishmen smile and sit down with them.)

THE PORTUGUESE

(entering) So, Mr. Corno, here's the famous garden of the Palais-Royal, so celebrated that even in Lisbon we know it almost as you.

DUCORNEAU

Not possible!

THE PORTUGUESE

Judge! Isn't that the Meridian Alley of the Rue des Enfants on which it's fashionable to adjust your watch?

DUCORNEAU

Astonishing.

BEAUSIRE

And opposite us, the site of the celebrated tree of Cracow, with the Café Foy, celebrated for its patroness, the beautiful Mme Jousseraud.

(low to Saint Landry) Where I still have an unpaid tab!

SAINT LANDRY

And as for me, I have a roof.

DUCORNEAU

Prodigious!

SAINT LANDRY

Still, aren't those galleries there constructed by the Duke of Orleans to the great displeasure of local owners, and in particular, Miss Sophie Arnould?

DUCORNEAU

Phenomenal! And to say that for the week I've been showing you Paris, it's always the same. Yesterday, leaving the performance at Audinots, I was lost in the Rue Ours. Well, this gentleman, the first secretary, set me on the right path.

BEAUSIRE

By Jove, it's my quarter.

(catching himself) My quarter by preference.

THE PORTUGUESE

By the way, Mr. Corno, do you know that today these merchants should bring us their definitive reply for the necklace?

DUCORNEAU

Why, tomorrow, Milord.

THE PORTUGUESE

I will do my part in high places for your good offices in this affair, Mr. Corno and we will try to reward them with a plaque of one of our national orders—

DUCORNEAU

(dazzled) Such an honor for me!

BEAUSIRE

(very dignified) Yes! Yes! But before returning, if His Excellency would care to taste a glass of Maraschino.

THE PORTUGUESE

My word, willingly, Corno.

(heading towards the back)

SAINT LANDRY

(stopping Ducorneau) No, not here! Opposite! It's better.

DUCORNEAU

That's true? How does he know?

AMARINTHE

Heavens! More English! Regent Street—Westminster.

SAINT LANDRY

(low to Beausire) Watch out! Amarinthe and Nina!

DUCORNEAU

Huh! They know them, too. Like the Rue Ours!

(They leave.)

CLELIE

(passing and talking with Sylvia) My first was a shepherd and yours?

SYLVIA

As for me, my sweet, my first lover was two soldiers.

RETEAU

(going to Nicolette) Well, pretty Nicolette, how's our Ettenoitna doing?

NICOLETTE

Marvelously! I don't know what's causing it. It's vain for the Parisians to adore the Queen—all the pamphlets against her sell like hot cakes. I've already sold all mine.

RETEAU

And one gentleman alone—the Count de Cagliostro has just bought 1,000 from me in one fell swoop!

NICOLETTE

The Devil! Now that's one who's starting a sale. For the moment, mine is almost finished, for dinner time is approaching.

RETEAU

Then, until tomorrow, Miss Nicolette.

(he sits at a table and the waiter comes to get his order)

COUNTESS

Ah! Mr. de Vilette—it seems this is always your habitual meeting place. But first of all, do you recognize me?

RETEAU

How could I forget the wife of the Count de la Motte, my old comrade in the men of the King—who so often obliged me with his purse although he was no better off than I—and he's in good health, this dear friend?

COUNTESS

Marvelous—but he's not what it's about at the moment. Do you still love money, Mr. Reteau?

RETEAU

Hey, Madame, it's the only love in life that never ends. Unfortunately, the ingrate doesn't pay me back.

COUNTESS

And do you still possess that remarkable calligraphic talent which got you kicked out of your regiment for having imitated too exactly, I think, the signature of your treasurer?

RETEAU

Still, Madame—when heaven has favored you with such gifts, isn't it honoring them to keep them in practice? But would you need to call on them?

COUNTESS

Perhaps.

RETEAU

You can count on my zeal because—

COUNTESS

—Because I know how to remunerate it as suits it, right? Don't worry, I won't regard the price—where are you living?

RETEAU

A short distance from here 28 Rue Bons-Enfants.

COUNTESS

That's fine, I will find you there this evening or tomorrow at the latest. For the moment, let's leave each other, for I am expecting someone I've given a rendezvous to and who ought not to see us together.

RETEAU

Countess.

(bowing) I am your servant.

(to Nicolette) What, you are already closing your shop, Miss Nicolette?

NICOLETTE

My word, yes, you see there's almost no one in the garden.

RETEAU

Then until tomorrow.

(They go off together.)

COUNTESS

(alone) On this side all is going well. There remains the cardinal. Here he is not satisfied with having a mysterious secret with the

Queen, and seeing his pretended accomplice before the whole Court, from sovereign to grand almoner. Ah, Monsignor— you must have a private meeting. Well, you shall have it—and finally, here's the one I've been expecting.

OLIVA

Madame Countess—

COUNTESS

Weren't you expecting me, my beauty?

OLIVA

So it really was you who wrote me this letter that the concierge of our former lodging brought me so mysteriously?

COUNTESS

Precisely! But how you have changed since those days! Without being indiscreet is it to Mr. Beausire that you owe these elegant finery?

OLIVA

Oh! No! I have a protector! A very rich and powerful. Lord! But you know him, the Count de Cagliostro.

COUNTESS

(surprised) Truly?

OLIVA

Oh! I cannot complain about him! He's very good to me. Jewelry, silks, outfits, he gives me everything I want. Only—

COUNTESS

Only?

OLIVA

He doesn't want me to put my nose outside and if he knew I disobeyed him by coming here, especially to the Palais Royal— he would be furious! He only let me go out once in the last two weeks, to go to the Place Vendome—to Mr. Mesmers.

COUNTESS

I wasn't mistaken.

(aloud) Ah! You went to Mesmer's?

OLIVA

Yes, last Tuesday. But that's enough to occupy ourselves about me. And you, Countess, you are speaking of my outfit? What shall I say of yours?

COUNTESS

It's that I, too—my position has really changed. The Queen has caused my rights to be recognized. She honors me with a quite particular affection—we are together like two fingers on the same hand.

(looking at her carefully) And yet—

OLIVA

Why are you looking at the whites of my eyes?

COUNTESS

It's precisely because of the business for which I want to speak to you. Imagine that Her Majesty has directed me to find a person who can do something that will be explained to her when its convenient. It's a question of a trick she wants to play on an officer of her house. I would be enchanted if your heart speaks to it—to make you profit by the godsend—for you would earn 15,000 pounds without counting the protection of Her Majesty.

OLIVA

Oh! I would be very happy to please the Queen so as to be guided by interest.

(Cagliostro has appeared. He hides behind the newspaper pavilion)

CAGLIOSTRO

(aside) Together! Thanks Countess, you are sparing me the pain of contacting you.

COUNTESS

For example, you must come dine at my place at Versailles this evening, for we will need a few days to prepare everything.

OLIVA

This evening—but Mr. de Cagliostro—

COUNTESS

So much the worse for him since he's not at the rendezvous?

CAGLIOSTRO

(hidden) Are you so sure of that, Madame?

COUNTESS

My carriage is nearby! And you will see how we will amuse ourselves. Is it agreed?

OLIVA

(laughing) Oh! My word! If we must amuse ourselves, I'm for it!

(They leave.)

CAGLIOSTRO

(alone) Come, I think my brothers in the Great Order will be satisfied with their Supreme Leader.

CHARNY

(entering) Pardon! Mr. de Cagliostro, I believe?

CAGLIOSTRO

The Count de Charny, it appears to me.

CHARNY

You know me?

CAGLIOSTRO

You know, sir, that I pass for a psychic. In my profession I must know everyone, even more reason to know Mr. de Charny, nephew of the Bailiff of Suffren, the right arm of Lafayette, the protege of the King—and the Queen.

CHARNY

Skip the charlatanism, sir, if you are psychic, so much the better for you; you then know why I am seeking you out, for I was going to go to your home and you can seek shelter in advance.

CAGLIOSTRO

(ironic) Shelter? And shelter from what, if you please?

CHARNY

Guess, if you are a psychic!

CAGLIOSTRO

So be it! To please you, you are coming to seek a quarrel with me?

CHARNY

If you know that, you doubtless know on what subject?

CAGLIOSTRO

Yes, sir—on the subject of the Queen?

CHARNY

You are right, sir—I have already chastised your accomplice, your turn now.

CAGLIOSTRO

You mean, sir?

CHARNY

I mean that I've just come from the home of Mr. Reteau de Villette, author of a brochure that appeared this morning against Her Majesty, the Queen, that I cudgeled this wise guy and that I forced him with blows from a cane to destroy all that he still possessed of his odious libel. But I learned from him that you bought a thousand copies and I intend to know where they are.

CAGLIOSTRO

I might reply to you that where they are is my business. I prefer to tell you they are at my place.

CHARNY

Sir, you appear to me to be a courageous man. Therefore I summon you to give me satisfaction for the insult done to the Queen, an insult which you are making yourself the accomplice of by detaining even one copy of this gutter sheet.

CAGLIOSTRO

Sir, you are in an error that pains me. I love novelties, scandalous rumors, ephemeral things. I collect them and it's as a collector that I bought that brochure.

CHARNY

A man of honor does not collect infamies.

CAGLIOSTRO

You are mistaken, sir, the pamphlet is not an infamy, because Her Majesty was at the Mesmer's tub.

CHARNY

That's false.

CAGLIOSTRO

(very calm) You want to say that I'm lying?

CHARNY

I don't want to say it. I said it! Well, didn't you hear me?

CAGLIOSTRO

I didn't miss a word of what you said to me, sir.

CHARNY

Don't you know what a lie is worth?

CAGLIOSTRO

(more and more calm) Yes, sir. There's even a proverb in France which says a lie is worth a slap in the face.

CHARNY

(furious) Then I am astonished, not to see your hand rise to my face and your sword emerge from its sheath.

CAGLIOSTRO

I only pay what I owe!

CHARNY

(more and more irritated) Watch out! You are going to expose me to take with you the same role I took with the gazetteer.

CAGLIOSTRO

(smiling) Ah! Blows with a stick—well, reflect in your turn, sir—you are going to approach me with your cane, I am going to take you by the back bone and I will toss you ten paces from me—and that understand plainly, as much as your heart will tell you of it.

CHARNY

(in a paroxysm of anger) Sir, if you are as strong as four street porters, there are other weapons for a gentleman. In that case, I repeat, sword in hand Count, or it is I who will slap you—sword in hand or you are dead!

CAGLIOSTRO

You insist on it, sir—so be it!

(The two men go on guard. Cagliostro disarms Charny.)

CHARNY

(furious) Damn it all!

CAGLIOSTRO

(coldly) Shall we start over?

(New battle, same result.)

CHARNY

(in a complete fury) Again.

CAGLIOSTRO

(giving his adversary back his sword) I'm waiting for you.

(After a short hesitation, Charny rushes on guard again. He is disarmed for a third time.)

CHARNY

Ah! Kill me, sir—kill me since you are the stronger!

CAGLIOSTRO

The stronger. Do you think it is the sword that makes one man stronger than another, Mr. de Charny? No, it's right, justice, truth.

CHARNY

Justice! I had that, for I was acting by virtue of a sacred principle.

CAGLIOSTRO

Which is?

CHARNY

I am defending the monarchy.

CAGLIOSTRO

You who went to America to defend the Republic!

CHARNY

Well, I am defending the Queen who's slandered. I am defending my Country, whose evil genius you are!

CAGLIOSTRO

(with a solemn authority) Who told you that? And where does this boldness to think you are right and I am wrong come from? You are defending royalty? Well, suppose that I am defending humanity? You say—give to Caesar what belongs to Caesar! I say. Give to God what belongs to God! Republican from America, I remind you of the love of men, of the love of equality. You step on nations to kiss the hand of Queens, as for me, I trample Queens underfoot to raise up nations! I do not trouble you in your adorations; don't trouble me in my work. I leave you the great day, the sun in the heavens and the sun of courts; leave me shade and solitude. You said to me, "You will die, you who have offended the object of my cult." I say to you, "Live, you who fought men" and if I say this to you, it's because I feel myself so strong, me and mine, that neither you nor yours can delay our progress for a minute!

CHARNY

(terrified) Sir, you overwhelm me. Perhaps I am the first in this country to foresee, thanks to you, a frightening future.

CAGLIOSTRO

Be prudent then, if you've seen the precipice.

CHARNY

Ah! I will throw myself in the chasm before seeing those I am defending fall into it.

CAGLIOSTRO

Well, I warned you, like the Prefect of Tiberius, I am washing my hands, Mr. de Charny.

CHARNY

(seizing Cagliostro's hand with feverish heat) Well, as for me— me—me—who am only a weak man and inferior to you—I will use against you the weapons of the weak. I will confront you, voice trembling, hands joined and I will soften you—I will get you to destroy this pamphlet which will make a woman weep— or on my honor, on this cult to which you alluded and that you know is more sacred to me than the whole world, with this sword impotent against yours, I will pierce my heart at your feet.

CAGLIOSTRO

(vanquished) Mr. de Charny, here's the key to the desk where all the thousand copies that you want are kept! Come with me, you will burn them yourself!

CHARNY

Oh! Thanks! A hundred times thanks!

CAGLIOSTRO

(very moved) Ah! Why aren't they all like you—I would be with them and they wouldn't perish.

## C U R T A I N

# ACT III

## SCENE 7: THE EMBASSY
## OF PORTUGAL

*A large salon with white but rather dilapidated wainscoting, in the Embassy of Portugal, rue La Jussienne. Spartan and faded furniture. Portraits of great Portuguese personality with solemn faces. Two small doors in cutaways. Two large side doors. A safe between the door and the window.*

*At Rise: Everyone is finishing lunch. They are eating every which way—seated on the ground, at tables, on the back of arm chairs, serving themselves with their fingers and drinking from bottles.*

BEAUSIRE

Hey, good, good, good—
How good wine is
I intend to drink it for my thirst!
Hey! Good! Good! Good!
How good wine is,
I intend to drink it by the liter!

(All those present, glass or bottle in hand, take up the refrain of the chorus.)

SAINT LANDRY

Another bottle.

COMMANDER

(as second valet) Pass me eau-de-vie.

PHILOSOPHER

(as a black cook) Give me the sweets!

BEAUSIRE

Gentlemen.

(same intonation—furious) Ah! Indeed! Will you shut up—bunch of drunks.

SAINT LANDRY

(finishing a pot of sweets with his fingers) What's the matter now?

BEAUSIRE

The matter is that it's quite nice to empty the bottoms of the bottles and sweet pots, but that we must busy ourselves a bit with our business.

PORTUGUESE

Mr. Beausire is right. That imbecile of a Ducorneau, who is lunching elsewhere, returns regularly at two o'clock. We've just got time enough.

L'ARTAIGNE

(mouth stuffed) Beausire—expose the situation.

ALL

Yes, yes.

BEAUSIRE

Gladly—gentlemen, up to now no obstacle has fettered our admirable enterprise. Thanks to our prudence, the agents of Mr. de Crosne have not put their nose in our business and if they are informed of it, it will be too late because we are awaiting the jewelers this afternoon and the necklace must make our fortune.

SAINT LANDRY

On this subject, the association insists that the safe containing the 100,000 pounds, the safe over there—(pointing to it)—not be situated exclusively in the apartments of the ambassador.

PORTUGUESE

Because it's Ducorneau who has the key to 'em.

SAINT LANDRY

Yes, but Mr. de Beausire has taken the imprint and had you make another.

BEAUSIRE

(protesting) Have a key made, me?

(aside) Actually, I had two made.

PORTUGUESE

It's in the interest of the association.

SAINT LANDRY

Agreed, but then each of us, having equal rights, equally demands a key to the safe.

ALL

(less Beausire) Yes, yes—

PORTUGUESE

I refuse.

L'ARTAIGNE

Why?

ALL

Yes, why?

PORTUGUESE

You distrust me—why shouldn't I distrust others? It seems to me if I can be suspected of stealing from the association, I can suspect the association of stealing from me.

ASSOCIATES

Oh! Don Marvel!

PHILOSOPHER

(furious) Us! Thieves?

L'ARTAIGNE

Withdraw the word.

ALL

Yes, yes, withdraw the word.

BEAUSIRE

(interposing) Gentlemen! Gentlemen!

(he rings a bell on the desk)

THE SWISS, THE COOK, THE OTHER VALET

(answering the bell) Here! Coming!

SAINT LANDRY

There we go!

BEAUSIRE

(profiting by the uproar) Ah! Gentlemen, discord is going to agitate its burning brands amongst us—when these 800,000 pounds have hardly a few hours—what shall I say—a few minutes to remain in their safe.

PHILOSOPHER

It's true.

L'ARTAIGNE

He's right.

BEAUSIRE

So, it's agreed, you are withdrawing your motion—

SAINT LANDRY

Since it's only a matter of minutes.

ALL THE ASSOCIATES

We withdraw it.

PORTUGUESE

Gentlemen, your confidence honors me.

BEAUSIRE

For the moment, trust me, let's continue until the last moment to care for our roles—and to make the embassy run on the Portuguese model, so they will say of us later, "If they weren't real ambassadors, they almost deserved to be!" It's always flattering!

(A bell rings twice behind the door.)

SAINT LANDRY

The bell.

PHILOSOPHER

It's Ducorneau returning.

PORTUGUESE

Let's clean up this mess.

BEAUSIRE

(to the Swiss, the 2nd Valet, the black cook) You are leaving—
get out!

(Saint Landry arranges the platters. The three junior valets
take away the dishes with food. The Portuguese sits at the desk
plunged in his papers—Beausire does the same at another table.)

DUCORNEAU

(entering timidly) Pardon—what, Milord, already working?

PORTUGUESE

(without leaving his papers) Always, Mr. Corno.

BEAUSIRE

Always.

DUCORNEAU

To set to work so soon after eating, it's very bad—it can lead to
a congestion. As for me, I have to wait for three or four hours
after each meal.

PORTUGUESE

(mouth full) I don't take time to lunch.

BEAUSIRE

(the same) Me either.

SAINT LANDRY

(the same) Me either.

DUCORNEAU

Not possible. Why what the caterer sent—

BEAUSIRE

The Ambassador had it distributed to the office.

DUCORNEAU

What a man! Do you know, Milord, that it's lucky for Europe—Portugal is a small state.

PORTUGUESE

Why, Mr. Corno?

DUCORNEAU

Because with geniuses like you at its head, it would grow quickly.

PORTUGUESE

But it is growing.

BEAUSIRE

Yes, it's growing.

SAINT LANDRY

Oh! Certainly, it is growing.

(Bell rings three times.)

DUCORNEAU

Three rings of the bell.

PORTUGUESE

Great—not more importunates.

SAINT LANDRY

(who's looked out the window) Milord, it's the jewelers.

DUCORNEAU

They are coming to bring the necklace.

PORTUGUESE

Stay, Corno, stay. You are not one too many.

SAINT LANDRY

(announcing) The gentlemen jewelers to the crown.

PORTUGUESE

Seats for these gentlemen.

(Saint Landry advances stools for Boehmer and Bossange)

BOSSANGE

(low to his partner) Speak, you—

BOEHMER

No, you—as for me, I don't dare.

BOSSANGE

Monsignor, if there's an act which cuts us to our hearts, a respect for the sovereign of the great nation that you so worthily represent, it's actually the communication that we are coming to make to Your Excellency.

BOEHMER

I was going to say that.

PORTUGUESE

(slightly uneasy) A communication?

BEAUSIRE

(low to Saint Landry) What does it mean?

SAINT LANDRY

(low) I don't understand.

BOSSANGE

(after hesitating) Monseigneur, to our great regret, to our real sorrow even, political considerations of the highest importance are preventing us from following through on the negotiations begun between us.

DUCORNEAU

(speechless) What are you saying?

BEAUSIRE

(stupefied) Is it possible?

SAINT LANDRY

What did I hear?

BEAUSIRE

Look here, gentlemen jewelers—you've found a bidder—well, must we offer you 50,000 pounds more?

BOSSANGE

Useless, Mr. Secretary.

PORTUGUESE

Fifty thousand, a hundred fifty thousand pounds.

BOSSANGE

No, sir, don't take the trouble of tempting us. A will more powerful than ours constrains us to sell the necklace in this country. We beg you to make Her Very Pious Majesty accept our very numerous excuses and to accept them yourself.

PORTUGUESE

(angry) That's fine, gentlemen, I won't keep you any longer.

BOSSANGE

(bowing; aside) Oof!

BOEHMER

I was going to tell him.

PORTUGUESE

Mr. Ducorneau—Ramírez, escort these gentlemen jewelers.

(They leave, escorted by Ducorneau and Saint Landry.)

PORTUGUESE

Everything is ruined.

BEAUSIRE

Completely!

PORTUGUESE

And the 108 thousand pounds in the safe, shared by the eight of us, gives each a total of—

BEAUSIRE

(who calculates on paper) Thirteen thousand, five hundred pounds.

PORTUGUESE

That's ruin! We've been cheated.

BEAUSIRE

Whereas if there were only two of us—

PORTUGUESE

Fifty four thousand pounds each.

BEAUSIRE

That's a consolation.

PORTUGUESE

But Saint Landry, who's going to come back will demand his share.

BEAUSIRE

Wait. I have a way. Here he is. Leave it to me, and say as I do.

SAINT LANDRY

(entering) Well! What a catastrophe!

BEAUSIRE

I bet you already told our associates.

SAINT LANDRY

No—no.

BEAUSIRE

Good—because if you had spoken, you would have committed a great stupidity and lost a great sum.

SAINT LANDRY

A great sum! How's that?

BEAUSIRE

Hell! Being only three to know the business failed—we could be the only three to share the 108 thousand pounds, since the other thing the jewelers took them.

SAINT LANDRY

(joyous) By Jove, it's true!

BEAUSIRE

Thirty-three thousand 303 francs, six sols per head.

SAINT LANDRY

More than the fraction of 8,000 pounds.

PORTUGUESE

So, you accept?

SAINT LANDRY

By Jove!

BEAUSIRE

(in a thundering voice) I told you, you were only a cheat! Come, Don Marvel, you who are robust, seize this wise guy for me and let's hand him over to our associates.

(The Portuguese leaps on Saint Landry.)

SAINT LANDRY

(half choked) Mercy! Mercy! I was joking!

BEAUSIRE

First of all gag him.

(he places his belt around his mouth)

PORTUGUESE

Where to stash him?

BEAUSIRE

There—in the black cabinet! In the back of this corridor.

(Opening the small side door at the right, the Portuguese goes in carrying Saint Landry in his arms.)

PORTUGUESE

(in the corridor) Wait! I locked him in!

BEAUSIRE

(looking the key in the door on the Portuguese) And as for me, I'm also locking you in—let's see—the other door now.

(he successively locks all the doors) One! Two! Three! It's not just locking everything; we must open—

(opens the safe and removes the money) —And especially to show a clean pair of heels for the police won't be slow to meddle in our affairs. Not counting the week we were ambassadors the true Marquis de Souza can't be far away.

(Shocking uproar at each of the four doors.)

ASSOCIATES

(behind the doors) Open! Open!

BEAUSIRE

(looking at the doors) Real oak! I've got time!

ASSOCIATES

(beating with redoubled blows) Open—open the door.

BEAUSIRE

No, gang—I'm opening the window.

(He opens the window, sticks his leg over the balustrade and disappears. Shocking tumult behind the doors which are being beaten by blows of hammers and hatchet. Simultaneously, they all four fall open at once, dragging in their fall the Portuguese, Saint Landry, L'Artaigne, the Philosopher, the Commander, Positive and Le Grigneaux, who immediately get up.)

PORTUGUESE

Where is the wretch?

SAINT LANDRY

(pointing to the window) Stolen off, by Jove!

(Portuguese voice of the Portugese Mace- bearer in the corridor)

VOICE

Open to the Marquis de Souza, Ambassador of Portugal.

PORTUGUESE

The true Ambassador.

DUCORNEAU

(entering) Marquis! Mr. Secretary!

PORTUGUESE

(pushing him away) No more secretary!

SAINT LANDRY

(pulling off his wig) No more Marquis.

(three blows are struck on the door below)

PORTUGUESE

(after looking out the window) Save yourself, if you can.

(General flight by the window and side doors. From the door at the left in cutaway enter a black usher—smooth shaven, preceding a very old, very ugly lord who seems like a walking portrait.)

USHER

(in a cavernous voice) The Marquis de Souza, Ambassador of Portugal.

DUCORNEAU

(standing up, completely bewildered) The Marquis! Ah, swine, I've got you.

(He rushes the old lord behind whom has entered a cortege as solemn as it is numerous and belabors him with his fist. Tableau.)

**CURTAIN**

# ACT III

## SCENE 8: THE BATHS OF APOLLO

*A square in the Park of Versailles before the grove named the Baths of Apollo. At the back of the stage, but within the sight of the spectator, ruins a sort of Greek temple which is reached by a rustic bridge thrown over a stream of water that emerges from a grotto and a natural cascade, at the spectator's left. To the left, the wall of the park pierced by a small gate which the foliage renders almost invisible. To the left, in the trees can be distinguished the roof and top floor of a small house completely enveloped by foliage, whose shutters are closed. Nine o'clock at night—summer night at the beginning then, moonlight.*

*King and the Count de Provence—coming from the rear.*

COUNT

I am truly charmed by this stroll, thanks to which I've been able to prove to Your Majesty that far from being ill disposed toward the Queen, I am, to the contrary, her devoted servant and her respectfully affectionate brother.

KING

I never doubted, brother. Nor did she.

COUNT

If you know how delighted I was that the unfortunate squabble of the other day has been clearly explained.

KING

(sighing) And me, too.

COUNT

(calculatingly) In the end, all was for the best, at least as far as that affair with Mesmer—

KING

Yes, but—could there still be another affair? Explain yourself, I beg you.

COUNT

There! There! Don't get upset—the adventure with the carriage, by Jove. But that's an old story. Because it dates from last winter. It's true that the mystery has only been recently clarified. It's Laurent—the gardener—concierge of the small gate who insists that one evening or rather one night toward the end of March, the Queen went out around eleven with Weber and one of her women that he was unable to recognize and didn't return until after midnight in a cab escorted by a young officer of very fine appearance, to whom Laurent heard that she was giving herself and her companion out as two of the palace linen drapers with night leave time.

KING

And did he know this officer?

COUNT

Actually, he didn't know him at the time when this story took place but since then, he's been quite surprised to see him again and to see him frequently, since this officer suddenly became an aide de camp of Your Majesty and one of the most assiduous familiars of the Queen.

KING

His name? His name? I tell you!

COUNT

The Count de Charny!

KING

The Count de Charny! Truly! The invention is for too clumsy. It was I myself who presented him to the Queen barely a week ago, at Trianon, Mr. de Charny was coming from India.

COUNT

Sire—it's not I you must accuse, but this caitiff of Laurent.

KING

To have deceived me to this degree, it's impossible!

COUNT

And hold on, there he is right now just making his round to turn off the fountains just like every night. If it pleases, Your Majesty to question him—

KING

No.

(They leave.)

(The Retreat can be heard played on drums and the music of the French guards. It crosses the stage and then fades into the distance where it decreases little by little. Night comes on. The Bailiff de Suffren and Charny enter from the right.)

CHARNY

The retreat is over. We no longer risk meeting anyone in the park, Come, Uncle.

SUFFREN

Finally you are going to explain to me the reason for this confinement you are condemning yourself to?

CHARNY

Sadness—boredom—weariness—one has moments like that in life.

SUFFREN

Oliver, I know you! For three years we've lived between the sea and the sky, under the eye of God. Oliver, my child, you have a passion in your heart—an unhappy passion.

(silence) You are going pale, you are trembling. You see plainly I've guessed it.

CHARNY

Well! Yes, it's true! My life is a shocking torture. Ah! God! You don't know what it is to love a woman to distraction, passionately—madly and to be certain, absolutely certain, you hear, whatever happens, she will never be yours.

SUFFREN

She's married?

CHARNY

(with growing passion) Ah, if ever a married woman, if ever I loved her with that savage love which makes you forget everything, I would say to that woman, "Come! There still remain some beautiful days for us on Earth! Those that await us outside of love—what good are they?" But alas, if she were to consent, if she were capable of consenting to follow me—-she would never leave her children! Still, children can be carried away in the bottom of a traveling cloak. See, Charny, since you are carrying off the mother in your two arms without feeling anything but a shiver of love, wouldn't you carry off her children, too?

(with terror) Aloo! The children of a king, it's so heavy, that one would feel emptiness in half the world.

SUFFREN

Wretch! Well, it's no longer your father who begs you, it's your Captain who commands you, you will leave tomorrow.

CHARNY

(with anguish) Ah! Don't force me never to see her again.

SUFFREN

Now I understand why you live in this house!

CHARNY

(adoringly) Well, yes, it's so as to be near her! Sometimes behind my closed blinds, I see her pass, I hear her laugh, and a ray illuminates my night. Then, when she is gone, when the Retreat has separated all the world, as in this moment, I descend, I retake the path she took, I pick up a flower from the bushes where she stopped, I kiss the roses touched by her fingers.

SUFFREN

This is more than delirium! It's a terrible, mortal danger which threatens you, for the secret that you are carrying within you is one of those that kill. I insist that you execute my orders.

SUFFREN

That's fine! I will obey.

SUFFREN

Tomorrow I will come to find you myself and going to Brest where I will remain with my squadron. I will embark you. Now lead me back.

CHARNY

This door opens on an alley which abuts the boulevard. They gave me a key to it when they rented the house to me.

SUFFREN

Are you accompanying me?

CHARNY

Surely!

(He opens the door.)

SUFFREN

(extending his arms into which Charny throws himself) Ah! My poor child, I will cure you, go!

(They leave.)

(Again one hears in the distance the sound of Retreat. Enter Andrea de Taverney sad and dreamy.)

ANDREA

A week he hasn't appeared at the palace. She made a remark about it just now at cards. The Queen—? Why am I haunted by that idea? Jealousy. I am jealous of the Queen! So then it's true, Andrea de Taverney, the Wise—as I am called, love the Count de Charny! And he doesn't suspect it. He will never suspect it. If he knew, Great God! It seems to me I would die of shame. Oh, my head is on fire—the coolness of this mild night will calm me.

(She goes into the alley at the back.)

ANDREA

Everything is sleeping in the palace, even Her Majesty. As for him, he's in love with the Queen—! No, that cannot be. That's not it!

(She disappears behind the trees.)

CHARNY

(returning through the small gate at the right) My uncle's right. I will leave tomorrow. That's the only way. More, more—I will never see you anymore. I will no longer see, as in this moment, like eerie night, the pale light shining behind your window which lights your precious sleep. But it seems to me I hear noise. People! At this hour in the park. Two women! Who can it be?

(He hides behind a thicket of trees at the right. From the same side enter Oliva and the Countess de la Motte. Oliva is dressed exactly like the Queen was at the Locksmith's! They arrive in a ray of moonlight. He recognizes them.)

CHARNY

The Queen! Ah! I will then see her once more for the last time. Why isn't she alone? I will brave all the tortures of falling at her feet.

COUNTESS de la MOTTE

Oliva, you remember all my instructions exactly?

OLIVA

To the letter, but this dress, this hair do, like that of the Queen— it's not to offend Her Majesty?

COUNTESS de la MOTTE

Child that you are! Since it's a game organized by the Queen herself—she saw you already, just now, and she was enchanted by you.

OLIVA

Truly?

COUNTESS de la MOTTE

And she will tell you with her mouth because she is behind that arbor!

OLIVA

(delighted) The Queen will speak to me. Oh! What a shame that my relatives are not here.

COUNTESS de la MOTTE

As to the one you are going to see—

OLIVA

This officer of ship's rigging who's in love with the Queen and that she wants to play the trick on.

COUNTESS de la MOTTE

Exactly—when he speaks to you, only reply to him as little as possible—wait—take this rose—

(She picks a rose from the bushes.)

CHARNY

(quietly, behind the trees) She is with Mme de la Motte-Valois—
but I cannot hear them.

COUNTESS de la MOTTE

You will give him this rose, adding only, "Here, let the gift of
this flower efface the past."

OLIVA

I will talk in a low voice the better to disguise my voice.

COUNTESS de la MOTTE

That's it. A key is turning in the lock—that's him—let's hide a
moment in the shelter of this bush.

(The Countess pulls Oliva into the shadow at the left of the stage
behind some bushes.)

CHARNY

(to himself) To what intrigue are they delivering themselves?

(The small gate at the right opens discretely. The Cardinal
appears completely enshrouded in a great cloak, hat pulled
down over his eyes. Reteau in somber livery as his valet.)

CHARNY

(from his hiding place) Two men.

CARDINAL

(mysteriously) You are in the service of the Countess?

RETEAU

Yes, Monsignor. And it's here she's expecting you with the person you know.

CHARNY

(to himself) What's this mean?

COUNTESS de la MOTTE

(emerging on tiptoe) I am here.

ROHAN

Ah! Countess be forever assured of my gratitude.

COUNTESS de la MOTTE

Her Majesty is nearby. Don't worry, I am watching over your safety.

(she leads him toward Oliva, hiding in the shadow, as the Cardinal bows with infinite respect)

CHARNY

(to himself) A rendezvous! Could this be a rendezvous? Why yes, what could she be coming to do in the park at this hour—? What's this man coming here to do?

ROHAN

(to Oliva) Ah! Madame, could all my life ever pay for the happiness that the Queen deigns to grant me?

OLIVA

(mysteriously) Here! Let the gift of this flower efface the past.

(she extends the rose to him)

COUNTESS de la MOTTE

Move away, Monsignor! Someone could be passing by.

(Oliva and Rohan slowly separate. They can be seen to pass over the little bridge and stop in the ruins of the little Temple.)

CHARNY

No—it's not possible! She is not capable of such infamy! He's some courier from Vienna, a messenger from her brother, the Emperor. The King forbids her to receive him because he's angry with the Court of Vienna and she's talking to him in secret. Yes—yes—that's it. Oh! To see! I want to see.

(He climbs the rocks over the cascade by the right; he hides behind the trees that are growing there.)

RETEAU

(to the Countess) You are sure that he doesn't recognize her?

COUNTESS de la MOTTE

Impossible. How could he suspect this astonishing resemblance?

COUNTESS de la MOTTE

Yes—the vengeance I am seeking,the weapon that can make the Queen go pale and confound the Cardinal—I've got it now! And since I don't have the power, since I don't have the love, at least I'll have a fortune.

CHARNY

(reaching the top of the cascade) I see her! He's leaning amorously over her shoulder—he's a lover! Mercy of God—he's a lover—ah! I intend to throw his guilt in his face.

(he rapidly climbs the length of the cascade)

COUNTESS de la MOTTE

Someone is coming.

(she runs to the bridge) Quick, Madame, come—it's the King.

(the two women turn sharply and sneak out)

ANDREA

(appearing from behind a tree) The Queen!

CHARNY

(on the bridge) It was indeed, she, but those two men—they were able to flee this way. Ah! I will find them.

(he rushes madly back to the left)

ANDREA

Him!

(she leaves shaking—by the right)

(Reteau, who has hidden with the Cardinal at the top of the cascade in the statues at the right.)

RETEAU

Let's leave, Monsignor! There's no longer anyone.

ROHAN

(emerging from his hiding place) You are right, they've succeeded in fleeing, no question. It's some park guard who frightened them, making his rounds.

(After a moment's glance in the direction of the false queen's flight, he heads rapidly to the gate at the left before which he finds Charny standing, arms crossed.)

CHARNY

No one leaves!

RETEAU

(aside, with hate) De Charny!

ROHAN

You are mad, sir—make way for me—I order it, I wish it.

CHARNY

You are imperious, sir—you are forgetting that only one single man, has the right to say I wish it—that's the King. And you are not the King! I must at least at all times believe it.

ROHAN

Sir, no more time. I have to pass. Don't you understand?

CHARNY

(overwhelmed with rage) And don't you understand that I won't let you through this gate without having seen your face—without knowing who is the man with whom the Queen is having a rendezvous at night?

ROHAN

Great God!

CHARNY

Don't you yet understand that if you want this passage, you must purchase it with your sword?

ROHAN

Sir, don't you know to whom you are speaking?

CHARNY

No, but I intend to know.

(he pulls off that hat the Cardinal had worn very down around his face) Cardinal de Rohan!

ROHAN

Mercy on me! The Queen is lost. This man is going to talk.

RETEAU

No! He won't talk.

(he strikes de Charny with a knife. Charny shakes, tries vainly to rise, and rolls at the feet of the stone bench)

ROHAN

(shocked) Wretch—what have you done?

RETEAU

It's my affair, Monsignor—I paid him back for his blows with a stick.

(He pulls the shocked Cardinal away.)

**CURTAIN**

# ACT IV

## SCENE 9: MARIE ANTOINETTE'S BOUDOIR

*The stage represents a room in the private apartments of the Queen at Versailles. Contemporary furniture, complete and sumptuous. Three large bays going to the ceiling occupy the back of the stage opening on a vast gallery. Facing the bay in the middle of the other side of this gallery, a large bronze door that of the palace chapel; two side doors. A small door to the oratory at the right, chimney on the left, bearing two Severs vases with large bouquets of lilies and roses—on the table, large bouquets of lilies and roses.*

*The ladies seated around are examining the Queen's jewels.*

QUEEN

I repeat to you, ladies that I will no longer put on these diamonds. It's natural that I am using them for the baptismal present that I must make to His Highness the Duke of Angouleme.

MME DE POLIGNAC

I've informed the Queen's jewelers and today they must bring her a design of the sword with a shoulder tie and buckles that Her Majesty desires.

QUEEN

Thanks.

(to Mme Campan, who enters) What is it, my dear Campan?

CAMPAN

It's Miss de Taverney, Madame—

QUEEN

Let her come in quickly! What she's going to announce now?

(Andrea enters dressed in black.)

QUEEN

(gaily) What ceremonies? Andrea.

(surprise) But why these dark clothes? Has something bad happened to you?

ANDREA

(very sad) A great misfortune, Madame—I am going to leave Your Majesty.

QUEEN

You're leaving? Then where are you going?

ANDREA

I no longer have a family, Madame. I have nothing to expect from earthly benefits and I am coming to ask Your Majesty's leave to occupy myself with my salvation.

QUEEN

What's the wrong headed decision mean, Andrea? Isn't the Queen the mother of a family who gives one back to those who have none?

ANDREA

Madame, your kindness penetrates me, but doesn't know how to dissuade me. I've decided to leave the court.

QUEEN

It's to Taverney you intend to go?

ANDREA

No, Madame, it's to the Abbey of St. Denis.

QUEEN

To a convent at your age! At twenty! Look, Andrea! I've loved you! I do love you! Don't leave me! It's humiliating to me, you know, to see a creature as perfect as you, abandon me.

ANDREA

(with a meaning the Queen cannot grasp) Humiliation doesn't reach faces as high as yours, Madame.

QUEEN

I seek vainly for something that has injured you.

ANDREA

Nothing has injured me, Madame.

QUEEN

And if I order you to stay?

ANDREA

I would be sorrowed to reply by a refusal to Your Majesty.

QUEEN

(with spite) That's fine, Miss—go to the convent in that case. Perhaps you have something to reproach yourself with? Why if you only did it for the ingratitude of which you are giving proof at this moment—you would be guilty enough. Go, Miss de Taverney—I still think you won't leave without taking leave of the King who holds you in particular esteem.

ANDREA

Your Majesty may be sure that I won't fail in that. Goodbye, Madame!

QUEEN

Goodbye!

(Andrea makes a deep curtsy and leaves) To leave like this without a word of tenderness—without a heartfelt outburst— without a kiss. Do you understand any of this, ladies?

MME DE POLIGNAC

Perhaps some thwarted love?

QUEEN

If she loves someone, why not name him?

MME DE LAMBELLE

Perhaps she is not loved.

QUEEN

Poor girl! Yes, perhaps—

MME DE LAMBELLE

Eleven o'clock—does the Queen permit us to go get ready for the Mass?

MME DE COIGNY

Today is the assumption.

MME DE POLIGNAC

And Cardinal de Rohan himself is officiating.

MME DE CHALONS

And there will be women at the Chapel!

QUEEN

Poor Cardinal! Well, I have lost all the prejudices I had against him. He has some good, ladies, let's go, till later.

(The women bow and leave by the rear. Mme Campan enters from the left.)

MME DE CAMPAN

It's His Majesty's jeweler—Mr. Bossange.

QUEEN

Show him in!

(Mme Campan introduces Bossange and leaves.)

QUEEN

Come forward, Mr. Bossange. Well, these designs?

BOSSANGE

Here they are, Madame.

QUEEN

(taking the designs) Think that these jewels are destined for the son of Count de'Artois.

BOSSANGE

They will be quite beautiful, Madame.

(in a low voice) No doubt, less beautiful than the Queen's necklace.

QUEEN

(smiling) Always that famous necklace. Haven't you yet sold it, my poor friend, because you are still thinking about it.

BOSSANGE

(looking around him) But it seems to me that Madame—only one is always occupied by such a jewel when one would want to see the one that buys it wearing it. And our business is so difficult, that we must especially think of it since it is not yet entirely paid for.

REINE

Those to whom you sold it have not yet paid you, Bossange? Well, they must do like me, let them return them to you, leaving the down payment.

BOSSANGE

(very uneasy) Huh? Your Majesty's not doing me the honor of saying she returned the necklace to us?

QUEEN

(calmly) Well, yes, I am saying it, what's wrong with you?

BOSSANGE

(very anxious) Returned? That's right, "returned" the Queen just said?

QUEEN

(severely) Ah, indeed! What kind of comedy are we playing?

Happily, I have wherewith to refresh your memory.

(she goes to her tallboy and pulls out a paper) For you are a very forgetful man, Mr. Bossange, so to say nothing further that's disagreeable.

(she hands him the receipt, which he examines, stupefied) Well, do you recognize the receipt, which attests you've retaken the necklace, and at least, you also haven't forgotten what your name is.

BOSSANGE

(lost) But Madame, it's not I who signed this—neither I nor my partner.

QUEEN

(stupefied in her turn) You deny it?

BOSSANGE

Absolutely! Were I to leave here my freedom, my life here, were the scaffold, were the executioner here, I would reply once again to Your Majesty, "No, no, no, this receipt is not from us."

QUEEN

(trembling) Then I've stolen from you? I still have your necklace?

BOSSANGE

(opening his portfolio) I don't think that if Your Majesty had wanted to return the necklace to us, she would have written this receipt here.

QUEEN

(seizing the paper Bossange offers her) What's this scrap of paper? I never wrote that! Is that my signature?

BOSSANGE

It's signed.

QUEEN

Signed Marie-Antoinette of France. But I don't sign "of France" I am an Archduchess of Austria, and you know very well that's how I sign all my papers? Come on, Mr. Bossange, the trick is too clumsy. Go tell it to your forgers!

BOSSANGE

(choked) My forgers!—Your Majesty suspects me—Bossange?

QUEEN

(haughtily) Actually, you suspect me, Marie Antoinette?

BOSSANGE

(crazed) Madame! Madame! How can Your Majesty suppose such things! If there escaped from me something that has displeased the Queen, may she forgive me. I am at her feet—but let her realize that this catastrophe is ruining us, destroying us, killing us!

QUEEN

Look—let's proceed calmly—you say you no longer have the diamonds?

BOSSANGE

No, Madame.

QUEEN

Didn't you see the Countess de la Motte-Valois? Didn't she remit to you on my behalf 200,000 francs?

BOSSANGE

No, Madame—the Countess said to us, merely "wait."

QUEEN

Then you didn't receive any money?

BOSSANGE

Pardon me, Madame, 500,000 pounds.

QUEEN

(altered) 500,000 pounds, and from whose hands?

BOSSANGE

From the Cardinal de Rohan.

QUEEN

Cardinal de Rohan.

(trying to pull herself together) Well, Mr. Bossange, from the moment that Cardinal de Rohan and I are mixed up in this business—you don't have to despair.

(calling) Mme Campan.

(Mme Campan enters.)

QUEEN

Let's someone go immediate to fetch Mlle de la Motte-Valois!

MME DE CAMPAN

She hasn't appeared in the palace since the day before yesterday, Madame.

QUEEN

All the more reason! Would you also inform the Cardinal de Rohan, who must be preparing for the ceremony, to come immediately.

(to Bossange) Go, and don't worry, Mr. Bossange, your case is in the hands of the Queen of France.

BOSSANGE

I humbly thank, Your Majesty.

(bows and leaves escorted by Mme de Campan)

MME DE CAMPAN

(returning) There's a Mr. de Charny, Madame, who begs the Queen to grant him a short audience.

QUEEN

Mr. de Charny! At this moment! Well, show him in.

(Mme de Campan introduces de Charny and leaves.)

CHARNY

(dressed in very somber velour) Madame. I've already once had the honor of asking Your Majesty's permission to leave the court. I am coming anew today to beg the Queen to render me my liberty.

QUEEN

Leave! You are requesting to leave, you too?

CHARNY

Yes, Madame, for the New World to rejoin Mr. de la Perouse.

QUEEN

Mr de la Perouse? Don't you know they say that Cagliostro prophetized to him he would not return.

CHARNY

That's why I want to go rejoin him.

QUEEN

To die! You want to die! But your devotion that I had accepted, your fidelity on which I was counting—you would deprive me of it? God knows if I still have need of it.

CHARNY

Your Majesty has only to choose among the faithful, among the devotees, she won't even notice my absence.

QUEEN

I still thought that you said, Mr. de Charny, that there are rare flowers that don't sprout in the sun of courts.

CHARNY

Yes, it's perhaps not the sun that makes them flower, perhaps they are born under the pale heaven of night to the mysterious flickering of stars.

QUEEN

I don't understand you—

CHARNY

(with distraction) Ah, Madame, I am a fool! But, my folly has devoured me for a long while. Were my head to fall off, I must speak. Yes, I dared to love, to love from the nothingness from which I sprang an exquisite creature, sacred—divine—a Queen—and my love was such that I would have died at her feet rather than let her suspect it. Suddenly, two days ago, my idol collapsed and broke into a thousand pieces. I saw that the Queen was only a woman, and that the wretch who adored her had to cast at her an accusation of shame and disloyalty.

QUEEN

(trembling) Mr. de Charny, you are insulting me! You are insulting the King, my master. Another word and I will have you driven out by my guards.

CHARNY

Well, in that case, I am going to say it before being driven out—

why for me death would be the sweetest of kindnesses. Day before yesterday, I was in your park, Madame, I saw you with that man, when you gave him the rose, saw when he kissed your hand, saw, when with him you went into the baths of Apollo.

QUEEN

(stupefied) Me!

CHARNY

(in despair) You! You! You!

(he staggers under emotion)

QUEEN

Look, sir, reply: You saw me in the park?

CHARNY

As I am seeing you! Wait. Don't I see you? You were wearing your green dress with gold silk train. I am dying of sorrow in saying to you. On my life, on my honor, it was you, Madame, it was you!

QUEEN

(very agitated) If I took an oath. If I swore on my son?

CHARNY

Ah, Madame, for pity's sake, don't take that oath for the proof of what I am asserting is that your companion's valet tried to kill me.

QUEEN

Is it true? Why, yes—that pallor! Sir, sit down because you are going to fall.

CHARNY

No! It seems that death hesitates before a soldier accustomed to look it in the face. But don't worry, I will succeed in deciding it.

QUEEN

Ah! Don't talk like that! My God! My God! And it's you, you who are accusing me of adultery. It's not enough that just now they are accusing me of theft.

CHARNY

Of theft?

QUEEN

Yes—remember that necklace that I'd refused the King in the past? Well, forgetting that when one is Queen, one doesn't have the right to a feminine caprice. I reconsidered that refusal—and I accepted the offer of Mr. de Rohan to purchase it in my name until I was able to pay him for it myself.

CHARNY

Mr. de Rohan?

QUEEN

Luckily, reason returned to me and I returned the necklace to the jewelers. And now, today, they insist they haven't received it! Oh! Lost, I need some light, some light and I will have it.

CHARNY

Madame, it's no longer a question of me! What is my suffering, what is my life compared to the honor and peace of Your Majesty? Trust me, avoid the uproar, the scandal if you don't want that tomorrow—the court, Paris, Europe—to repent that.

QUEEN

Get to the point.

CHARNY

Eh! Madame, that Mr. de Rohan paid for this necklace for the Queen, that Mr. de Rohan is the lover of the Queen!

QUEEN

Mr. de Charny, you are forgetting—

CHARNY

No, Madame, I am not forgetting anything, for the man I saw in the Park, the man with the rose, the man in the thicket, the man whose valet tried to murder me—it was Mr. de Rohan.

QUEEN

(terrified) Mr. de Rohan!

CHARNY

Madame, I beg you to listen to me, for this is the supreme moment. Straight to the enemy as in our battles. Straight into danger! Here, Madame, see a brother in me. This necklace is worth six hundred thousand pounds. From here in an hour—on my estates, I will have them accept them.

QUEEN

Mr. de Charny—you are a noble heart! I refuse.

MME CAMPAN

Does Her Majesty wish to receive Cardinal de Rohan, grand almoner of France?

QUEEN

Show him in.

(Mme Campan leaves.)

CHARNY

What are you going to do?

QUEEN

You said it, Mr. de Charny, straight to the enemy, straight into danger. Go in here.

(she points to the small door at the right) In my oratory, and leave the door ajar so as to be able to hear. Because before justifying myself in the eyes of the world, I intend to be pure in your eyes, Mr. de Charny, pure as the lily of France which has become my emblem.

MME CAMPAN

The Cardinal de Rohan.

ROHAN

(bowing very deeply) Your Majesty honors me by commanding me to her?

QUEEN

Yes, sir, you know what's happened on the subject of this necklace?

ROHAN

I just learned it—from the mouth of Bossange, Madame.

QUEEN

Then will you please give me positive information because for me, I no longer understand. First of all, where is this necklace that I returned to the jewelers?

ROHAN

(very surprised) The necklace that Your Majesty returned?

QUEEN

Yes, what have you done with it?

ROHAN

Me? Why—I don't know, Madame.

QUEEN

Look here, Cardinal, allow me to put suppositions in the place of shadows. Madame de la Motte-Valois intended to return the necklace. You whose kind idea of purchasing it for me, you persevered in this desire and you haven't returned it to the jewelers so as to return it to me on some occasion. Is that it? Have I reconstructed the affair? Tell me yes? Allow me to reproach you for this frivolity, this disobedience and all will be over. But for pity sake, for clarity, sir? I don't want at this moment that it cast a shadow over my life. Do you hear—I don't wish it.

ROHAN

Madame, I am going to reply to all of your suppositions. No, I did not persevere in the idea of making you keep the necklace, because I was assured that it was in your hands—no, I no longer have it because the jewelers don't have it because you yourself have it.

QUEEN

This is not possible! You don't have the necklace?

ROHAN

No, Madame.

QUEEN

And Madame de la Motte-Valois, who alone could inform us has disappeared. Where is she?

ROHAN

(with precaution) Since the moment I saw her the day before

yesterday with Your Majesty. Does no one know what has become of her?

QUEEN

Huh? You said day before yesterday? Who's speaking of the day before yesterday, sir?

ROHAN

(in a low voice) May Your Majesty forgive me if I permit myself to speak aloud my soul's secret, a secret of which she willingly accepted the confidence already.

QUEEN

(stupefied) A secret between us.

ROHAN

It is possible that Your Majesty doesn't remember?

QUEEN

No, sir, I remember nothing, you hear, nothing. Explain yourself completely—

ROHAN

Oh! Madame, why isn't the Countess here? She would help me, she, our friend, to awaken, if not the attachment, at least the memory of Your Majesty.

QUEEN

(sharply) Our friend? My attachment? My memory? Ah, indeed,

Cardinal, are you in your right mind?

ROHAN

Ah, Madame, free to no longer love you; don't be offended .

QUEEN

(going pale) Ah! My God! What's this man saying?

ROHAN

(getting excited bit by bit) Madame, I thought to have been suffi-ciently reserved so you wouldn't mistreat me—yet, it's true, I'm wrong. I ought to know that when a Queen says "I no longer wish it" it's a law as imperious as when a woman says, "I want it!"

QUEEN

(uttering a little scream and grasping the Cardinal by his lace sleeves) Answer quickly, sir, I said "I want it" to whom?

ROHAN

Why, to me.

QUEEN

(surrendering to fury) You are a wretch, sir!

ROHAN

Me!

QUEEN

You are a coward; you are slandering a woman!

ROHAN

Me?

QUEEN

You are a traitor, you insult the Queen!

ROHAN

(in his turn, no longer controlling himself) Me, Madame! Why was it I who dared to ask you for a nocturnal audience in your park?

QUEEN

(aside) My God! Charny was right.

ROHAN

Is it I who ever have dared to implore this flower—here—

(he pulls it from his breast) Adored, rose, accursed rose—dried, burned with my kisses!

QUEEN

(tearing it from him and trampling it underfoot) Oh, enough! enough!

ROHAN

Were you forced to give me your sweet hands whose perfume still is devouring my mind? Was it I, who in my wildest pride would have ever dared to dream on that heavenly blue night of sweet silences, of perfidious amours?

QUEEN

(in her turn, making the Cardinal unconciously recoil before her) Sir! Sir! You are going to say, even here, that you are seeking to ruin me, that you have invented all these infamies—that you didn't come to Versailles the other night.

ROHAN

I came here.

QUEEN

You are dead if you keep up that talk.

ROHAN

A Rohan cannot lie. I came here.

QUEEN

One last time, confess that you could have been deceived, that all this was a slander, a dream, impossible, but confess that I am innocent, that I can be!

ROHAN

No!

QUEEN

You are going to deal with the King's justice since you decline the justice of God!

(The large door opens and the King appears in discussion with the Count of Provence and Mr. de Breteuil, who leave him when he heads toward the Boudoir of the Queen.)

ROHAN

Here is His Majesty, Madame, who's preparing to be part of the service at which I must officiate. Do according to your good pleasure.

(The King having entered, the large door shuts behind him.)

QUEEN

(going to the King) Sire, here's Cardinal de Rohan, who's saying quite incredible things. Would you please entreat him to repeat them to you.

KING

Is it about a certain necklace which Mr. de Breteuil was talking to me about?

QUEEN

About the necklace, yes, Sire!

KING

Then you purchased these diamonds, sir.

(silence by the Cardinal to Queen) Since, Mr. de Rohan doesn't wish to reply, you Madame? Did you buy it, yes or no?

QUEEN

No.

KING

There's the word of a Queen. Take care, Cardinal.

ROHAN

Sire, all that I can affirm is that I've never had this necklace. All that I can affirm is that it is within the power of someone who does not wish to be named and thus forces me to say to her this word from Scripture, "Let the wrong fall back on the head of the one who committed it."

KING

The battle is between you and him, Madame. One last time—do you have this necklace?

QUEEN

NO! On the honor of my mother! On the life of my son!

KING

(to Rohan) Then it's an affair between you and justice, sir, unless you prefer to rely on my clemency?

ROHAN

The clemency of Kings is made for the guilty, Sire, I prefer the justice of men.

QUEEN

But, still, sir, your silence leaves my honor in play.

(The Cardinal remains silent.)

QUEEN

Well, as for me, I won't shut up, for this silence seems to attest to a generosity I don't want. Know, Sir, that all the crime the Cardinal committed is not in the sale or in the theft of the necklace.

KING

(uneasy) What's that mean?

ROHAN

I beg you, Madame.

QUEEN

Sire, summon the Cardinal to repeat to you what he said to me just now in this place.

ROHAN

Madame, Madame, you are exceeding the limits!

KING

Huh? Who's talking to the Queen like this? It's not, I, I suppose.

QUEEN

That's it exactly, Sire—the Cardinal is speaking this way to the Queen because he pretended to have the right.

KING

You, sir—

QUEEN

Isn't it to have rights over a woman when you affirm you obtained a rendezvous at night from her?

KING

Madame.

ROHAN

For mercy's sake!

QUEEN

(no longer in control of herself) As for the rest, for this rendezvous, for this intrigue, Mr. de Rohan, talks of having an aide, an accomplice, a friend who will give us timely information as to the rest.

KING

Who's that?

QUEEN

Madame de la Motte-Valois, sir.

KING

My forebodings were justified in that case. Well, let's see her, this woman, let's question her.

QUEEN

Ask the gentleman about what he did to her. He has a great interest that she not be involved.

ROHAN

The others who made her disappear have even greater interest than myself.

KING

That's what we shall see! While waiting stay at Versailles, sir, until what I have decided.

(The Cardinal bows very respectfully to the King and Queen and leaves by the left.)

KING

And you, Madame, count on the justice of your spouse and your king.

(He leaves by the back.)

(The King gone, the Queen tries to struggle, vainly, against the tears which oppress her. She falls onto a sofa, in prey to a veritable crisis of nerves and tears.)

CHARNY

(running to her) Madame, Madame—for pity sake.

QUEEN

(rising proudly) Mr. de Charny, you are the only man who's ever seen me cry, you will forget about it!

CHARNY

Your Majesty will be obeyed.

QUEEN

Well, no! In the end, I am choking for being unable to open my soul to anybody. Charny, my friend, inspire me, guide me, I cannot see my way because I no longer know where I am going! Or perhaps, alas! I know only too well.

CHARNY

Madame, since Your Majesty, does me the honor of asking advice of me, I will speak in all frankness. There exists a guilty person more dangerous and more threatening than Mr. de Rohan. That odious woman, Madame de la Motte-Valois, vanished when her testimony could vindicate you completely! So then, it's in her pursuit you must run, at the same time as her accomplice, this false Queen of France who has compromised the honor, the majesty, the modesty of the true Queen!

QUEEN

Alas—where is the devoted one, ardent enough to make a ray of light spring forth into this night, a light in these shadows, truth amongst these lies?

CHARNY

That devoted person awaits only a word, a sign from Your Majesty.

QUEEN

What? This cursed Queen, this ruined woman, that opinion is going to judge, perhaps condemn, this unfortunate is finding a defender?

CHARNY

A servant who venerates her, and who is offering her all that remains of the blood in his veins to staunch one of her tears— that she has permitted him to contemplate.

QUEEN

(with joy) Mr. de Charny, a Queen has no other love than her King, her people, her children, and her heart, vast enough to contain all her subjects, is too narrow to contain one alone.

CHARNY

Alas, I know it! And that's why I must leave, that's why I must die. Ah! Why didn't the knife of that man do its work completely?

QUEEN

Die! You—! No! No! I don't wish it!

CHARNY

(casting himself at her knees) Ah, that word is worth my life a thousand times. May Your Majesty forgive the impious one who dared for a moment to suspect his God!

(Marie Antoinette gives him her hand, which he kisses—the King walks in.)

QUEEN

The King.

KING

What grace can you be asking of the Queen, Mr. de Charny, to be there at her knees?

QUEEN

(aside) A grace!

KING

(to Charny) Speak!

CHARNY

Sire!

QUEEN

(aside) On his knees, what can one ask on one's knees?

KING

I'm waiting.

QUEEN

(hesitating) Sire—it's that Mr. de Charny's request is a secret.

KING

There are no secrets from the King.

QUEEN

Well! Mr. de Charny wanted to obtain from me permission to get married.

KING

Truly.

(taken with jealousy) But in what way does Mr. de Charny need to solicit you, so humbly to get married, Madame? Isn't he of good nobility, rich and brave? Tell me then the name of the woman that Mr. de Charny wishes to marry—and I will answer for removing the difficulty.

QUEEN

It's still one of those difficulties you cannot conquer, Sire—it is of that sort.

KING

Look—what thing is impossible to the King?

CHARNY

Sire.

KING

It's the Queen I am questioning, Sir.

QUEEN

(aside, trembling) An idea! Ah, help, my God.

(seized by an idea) Ah!

(aloud) Sir, she that Mr. de Charny wants to marry is in a convent.

KING

In a convent! Indeed, it is difficult, even for a King to carry off from God to give to men. Look here—who is this woman that you love—sir—tell me?

QUEEN

Sire, here she is.

KING

Miss de Taverney.

ANDREA

(coming forward) Who's coming to express to you her gratitude for your kindnesses, Sire, before retiring to the Abbey of Saint Denis.

KING

Miss—you and yours have for a long time done much for me

and mine. Will you accept for your dowry the 500,000 pounds that was perhaps wrong to refuse to Her Majesty a few days ago, and agree to marry the Count de Charny?

QUEEN

(low) Andrea, save your Queen.

ANDREA

(after a short internal struggle) I accept, Sire, and thank you a thousand times for your kindnesses.

(low to the Queen) Ah, Madame, do my services deserve for you to give me your lover for a husband?

QUEEN

(low) Andrea, you are mistaken.

ANDREA

(low) I was at the Bathes de Apollo, day before yesterday, I saw you there—and him, too!

QUEEN

(low) Me!

KING

(taking a paper on which he's just written) This doesn't acquit me with you, Miss, but since we are keeping you—you will give me time.

(deep curtsy by Andrea. Then the doors at the back open,

the gallery fills with people. Clock bells ring in the distance.)
Madame, here's the hour of service, your hand.

## CURTAIN

# ACT IV
## SCENE 10: THE VERSAILLES CHAPEL

*The bronze door opens and reveals the inside of the chapel, brilliantly illuminated. The cortege of clergy has begun. Under the archepiscopal dais, dressed as a Cardinal, in the aperture of the first bay appears Cardinal de Rohan. At the same time, a detachment of Swiss guards led by Crussol appears at the left.*

QUEEN

(stopping abruptly and releasing the hand of the King) Eh, What! Sire, it's before this man you want me to kneel? It's he who will extend his hand to bless me.

KING

I promised you justice would be done. Have confidence in me.

(At the moment the Cardinal comes down to greet the King, Mr. de Breteuil goes to him. The cortege stops.)

BRETEUIL

Monsignor Cardinal de Rohan, Landgraf of Alsace, Prince of the Empire, Grand Almoner of France; in the name of the King, I arrest you!

ROHAN

Me, Sire!

(The whole court is on stage; he descends.)

ROHAN

And where are you taking me?

BRETEUIL

To the Bastille.

ROHAN

In my pontifical garb! Before the whole court! The scandal is immense. Sire, it will only be the heavier on the head it falls back on.

KING

This is the way it must be. Come, Madame, pray for the happiness of our newlyweds.

(Charny offers his hand to Andrea, who takes it, both follow the King and Queen. The cortege enters the chapel, while Rohan moves away, saluted with a sword by an officer leading a detachment of gaurds. Organs, bells.)

## CURTAIN

# ACT V

## SCENE 11: THE CABARET DE BANCELIN

*A square on the boulevards, Coach doors and house to the right. To the left, the restaurant de Bancelin, surmounted by its Sign.*

CHARNY

(entering with Cagliostro) Truly, Count, it's to the Cabaret Bancelin you are taking me?

CAGLIOSTRO

Precisely.

CHARNY

Have you forgotten the cruel cares I confided to you, and do you think I have the heart to come see the impure and loose woman parade here at this rendezvous?

CAGLIOSTRO

Mr. de Charny, what did you tell me two hours ago?

CHARNY

That yesterday Mr. de Breteuil asked the King for a week to bring him Madame de la Motte-Valois. But that my reason, my instinct screams to me there exists another woman to find, whose appearance alone will cleanse the one they accuse with infamous suspicion which soil her already. This other woman, this mysterious twin that you yourself saw at Mesmer's bath, and Mr. Rohan in the Park of Versailles, I've sworn to discover and I'm coming to beg you to assist me.

CAGLIOSTRO

Mr. de Charny, we are struggling for two opposing camps. Those for whom I work, have for a motto, Lilia pedibus destrue! Trample the lilies underfoot. I cannot then favor the adversaries I'm engaged to combat. Still, I esteem you, I love you and I want to be useful to you. Besides, the time has not yet come and the damage born by our enemies suffices for the first engagement.

CHARNY

Then you will come to my aide?

CAGLIOSTRO

Personally, no; but I'm going to uncouple in your presence, two bloodhounds, who in hunting one of their own account will be able to start the game you are looking for! I am not hiding from you, for example, that these accomplices, are villainous enough types.

CHARNY

What do I care so long as I reach my end?

CAGLIOSTRO

Then come taste the partridge and the cooking of my friend, Bancelin from there we can observe my wise-guys.

(They go in to the right.)

(Beausire disguised as a blind man with a large cap over his eyes and a stick with a dog to guide him. On his breast, "Blind R.E. 10 Ter".

BEAUSIRE

(sing-song) Have pity on a veteran who lost both his eyes at the battle of Fonteroy.

(stopping to have a look around him) Having on one side a pack of bloodhounds attached to my person with the animosity of thieves who have been robbed, and on the other side with the necessity of coming to seek a letter at my domicile in which Oliva cannot fail to indicate to me where to rejoin her, the profession of a blind man seemed to me the most suitable to put my persecutors off my track. Let's install ourselves on this milestone and await events.

(The porter emerges from the house and sweeps the area.)

BEAUSIRE

Ah! Balthezar, my porter, if he suspected his tenant were so near him.

PORTER

Heavens, a blind man—poor man! I am going to give him the remainder of my soup.

(goes back in)

BEAUSIRE

Eleven o'clock. The courier from the little post delivers letters at noon. If I were to go explore the neighborhood? Dear Oliva! What joy to know herself rich. And rich because of her Beausire! Ah! All the same it's good to be able to give money to women.

(leaving) Have pity on a poor blind man who lost—

(he wanders off)

PORTER

(with a bowl) Here, my good man! What, he's gone? My word, lets go put my soup back on the heat. Connoisseurs won't be lacking.

(The Portuguese and Saint Landry appear in rags. Both are blind—the first with a large plaster over his eye. The other with a bandage. Each of them is guided by a dog and one has a hanging cord that reads, blind—deprived of sight—on the other—blind by nose struck off.

PORTUGUESE

What decadence for a former ambassador!

SAINT LANDRY

And for his valet de chamber! Still, it's the only way to put our hand on the rogue of a Beausire.

PORTUGUESE

You think?

SAINT LANDRY

No question. Follow my reasoning. Oliva, he told us, disappeared several days ago—but she will certainly give him news of herself; it's vain for our scapegrace to play dead; he'll have to come get news.

PORTUGUESE

Well, it's agreed! Let's keep out of sight and keep our eyes open.

PORTER

(in the doorway) Heavens, there are two of them. I'm going to get two bowls, that's all.

(He goes back in.)

PORTUGUESE

Still, they're passing.

(he begins a litany) Help an unfortunate, deprived of the light of day.

SAINT LANDRY

Have pity on a poor blind man, who doesn't see any light.

BEAUSIRE

(in between them) Charity for a veteran who lost his sight at

Fonteroy.

SAINT LANDRY and the PORTUGUESE

A colleague, by Jove!

BEAUSIRE

(at the milestone at the right) Heavens, a colleague!

(to the milestone at the left) What, another one! It's astonishing that there are blind men in all quarters here.

(installing himself facing them) My word, since they don't see clearly, they will not be annoyed.

SAINT LANDRY

A real blind man! He won't disturb us!

PORTER

(with two bowls) Here, my friends.

(The Three blind men at the same time.)

PORTUGUESE

Compassion for a wretch deprived of the light of day.

SAINT LANDRY

Have pity on a poor blind man who cannot see clearly.

BEAUSIRE

Charity for a veteran who lost his sight at Fonteroy.

PORTER

What! There are three of them! Ah! Indeed! All the blind in Paris have given themselves a rendezvous here. Wait! I'm going to get a third bowl.

OLIVA

(to Portuguese) Since this imbecile has discovered us, we might as well speak.

BEAUSIRE

(aside) Since this cad has betraycd me    let's engage in conversation.

(aloud) Dear colleagues, have you been frequenting this quarter long?

SAINT LANDRY

No, this is the first time.

BEAUSIRE

Then you don't know if this place is good?

PORTUGUESE

Oh! It must be. Opposite the Cabaret de Bancelin.

BEAUSIRE

Ah! Here is the Cabaret de Bancelin?

PORTUGUESE

No question. Look at the sign above my head—it's thick enough.

SAINT LANDRY

(kicking him) Animal!

BEAUSIRE

Heavens! How did you see the sign since you are blind?

PORTUGUESE

Hum! 'Twas my guide who pointed it out to me. Yes, before I had a guide—an invalid with a sliver leg and a wooden nose. No—a wooden leg—anyway, he's dead so I've replaced him with a dog.

BEAUSIRE

Pardon, you mean a bitch.

(calling) Sweety! Sweety!

PORTUGUESE

Huh? How were you able to see that?

BEAUSIRE

The Devil! I—I—I smelled her! You know the blind have their

other senses very developed—with me, odors have unheard of development.

SAINT LANDRY

(aside) Hum!

PORTUGUESE

This is singular.

(aloud) Would it be indiscrete, colleague, to ask you how you became blind.

BEAUSIRE

Why not at all—it's inherited!

(pointing to sign) Blind R.E.1O. Ter.

SAINT LANDRY

Ah! Yes—

PORTUGUESE

That sign.

BEAUSIRE

Not possible. They are reading print! I am distrustful of these blind men.

PORTER

(entering) Hold on, here are your three bowls.

(Enter messenger.)

BEAUSIRE

Ah! And here's the postman.

PORTUGUESE and SAINT LANDRY

How did you figure that out?

BEAUSIRE

Me? I smelled him—the odor—my sense of smell.

POSTMAN

(to Porter) A letter for Mr. Beausire!

PORTER

(encumbered by his soups) Hold on!

(Postman places the letter between the Porter's teeth.)

BEAUSIRE

No—give it to me.

(he opens it quickly)

PORTUGUESE and SAINT LANDRY

Huh?

BEAUSIRE

(reading) "Bar sur Seine—on the esplanade—the white house."

PORTER

(stupefied) A blind man who knows how to read.

BEAUSIRE

I'm flying there.

PORTUGUESE

Stop!

SAINT LANDRY

No one can pass.

BEAUSIRE

That's what you think.

(He shoves his sign in the stomach of the Portuguese who falls, and trips up Saint Landry with his cane—but in sneaking out, the letter falls from his pocket.)

SAINT LANDRY and the PORTUGUESE

(on the ground) Foiled again!

SAINT LANDRY

(spying his letter) No—his letter.

PORTUGUESE

(reading with him) "Bar sur Seine—on the Esplanade."

SAINT LANDRY

The white house.

PORTER

(stupefied) What! They are reading too!

PORTUGUESE

Let's run!

(They move off.)

PORTER

And my three soups?

SAINT LANDRY

(in the distance) Eat 'em!

CAGLIOSTRO

(to Charny, appearing at the left) All yours, Count, here are your huntsmen on the track, try to arrive at the Talley ho!

**CURTAIN**

# ACT V
## SCENE 12: MISS
## OLIVA'S LUNCHEON

*Bar sur Seine. A corner of the garden of the country house of Madame de la Motte-Valois. Shaped bowers and groups of five trees planted in the French way, to the right of the house at the back an entry gate equipped with panels. To the left, a wall covered with climbers, tables and rustic chairs.*

RETEAU

I tell you, Countess, that for us to delay here is a serious imprudence and to have brought this girl here is one greater still.

COUNTESS

Didn't I have to put in safety all that I cling to from the munificence of the Queen and Cardinal? Didn't I have to give my husband time to carve up the necklace and to sell it in England? What else do we have to suspect? The due date for the jewelers' falls in two weeks. At that moment, we'll all be at sea making sail for America.

RETEAU

But will Oliva agree to follow us? To leave this Beausire of whom she never stops talking—oh—if you had listened to me.

COUNTESS

What would you have done?

RETEAU

What one does with a tool that has become useless, our sole danger, the only witness who can speak against us, against you, is the little girl. Suppress this Queen-for-an-hour, and the true Queen will struggle helplessly in an inextricable net, the evidence of which I defy her to get out of. Some drops from this flask in Miss Oliva's chocolate—of which she takes a cup every morning on waking and nothing will threaten our security further.

COUNTESS

But that disappearance will cause a scandal—if we are caught, Mr. de Crosne will get wind of the adventure and the dead will speak more loudly against us than the living.

RETEAU

Then, let's do better! Under pretext of making her regain her Beausire, let's invite the beauty to climb in the chaise de poste which I brought myself, take her to the neighboring forest, and there! The vultures will quickly disfigure a cadaver which is rotting behind a bush!

COUNTESS

Yes, that way would be more sure; but we don't have need to come to that. I will persuade Oliva that she must accompany us and tomorrow, we will be en route with her to the shelter from all danger.

RETEAU

May the devil hear you—but what's that?

COUNTESS

One would say the galloping of a horse.

RETEAU

They're stopping at the gate.

(The bell rings.)

CRUSSOL

(behind the gate) Open the name of the King.

COUNTESS

(low) In the name of the King.

RETEAU

What did I tell you? What's to be done?

COUNTESS

Open, by Jove—and confront the danger face to face—if it is a danger.

(Reteau opens. Crussol tethers his horse to the gate and enters.)

COUNTESS

Count de Crussol.

CRUSSOL

Myself, Countess, delighted to find you in health. I am charged with a message for you on the part of Her Majesty.

COUNTESS

For me! What's it all about?

CRUSSOL

The Queen, I believe, needs your offices for she has had you looked for everywhere for the last four days. At your residence in Paris, we learned at last of your retreat and Mr. de Breteuil dispatched me at full gallop to beg you to return without delay at the wishes of the Queen.

COUNTESS

I am at Her Majesty's orders. But do you suspect why she needs me?

CRUSSOL

Not at all, Countess—unless it concerns this mysterious affair of the necklace.

COUNTESS

Necklace?

CRUSSOL

What's true? Here you can still know nothing. Imagine, Countess, the most twisted possible machinations in the world—in which until now only one thing is actually certain—

the arrest of Cardinal de Rohan.

COUNTESS

The Cardinal has been arrested?

CRUSSOL

And taken to the Bastille. I will tell you all this on the way for Mr. de Breteuil has directed me to proceed with the greatest rapidity and I've ordered at the post station a carriage that awaits us.

COUNTESS

The time to throw a cloak over my shoulders and I am with you.

(Rosalie brings lunch) But really, won't you take something? You see, they are serving me lunch.

CRUSSOL

In that case, Madame, a glass of water?

COUNTESS

(serving him) You will give me time to leave some orders with my intendant?

CRUSSOL

What do you think?

(The Countess says a word to Rosalie, who leaves, then approaches Reteau.)

RETEAU

Well? Have you made up your mind?

COUNTESS

(Loudly) Is it necessary?

RETEAU

Do you prefer the whip on the Place de Grave and the mark with hot iron at the hand of the executioner?

COUNTESS

(terrified) No—no—never.

RETEAU

(low) Then leave it to my doing—I will answer that she won't speak.

COUNTESS

But you must hasten.

RETEAU

In two hours we will have nothing more to fear.

(Rosalie brings a cloak and traveling shawl)

COUNTESS

(tossing the mantle on her back) Now, Mr. de Crussol—whenever you wish.

CRUSSOL

But, Countess, your lunch.

COUNTESS

(quickly) We will lunch en route, since the Queen is waiting for us.

(to Reteau before leaving) I am counting on you, sir.

RETEAU

(bowing) All your orders, Countess, will be rigorously executed.

(The Countess and de Crussol leave.)

RETEAU

(as Rosalie shuts the gate) Oliva vanished, I defy the Queen to get out of it. Let's see! We'll act quickly.

(writing in his notebook) All that remains is to order a carriage.

(to Rosalie) Rosalie quickly take this note to the inn where the post stops.

ROSALIE

Fine, sir.

RETEAU

(pulling a flask from his pocket) And as two precautions are always better than one—let's prepare Miss Oliva's lunch at all cost.

(puts a few drops of poison in the chocolate)

OLIVA

(yawning and stretching her arms, emerges from the house) It's amusing—the more you sleep, the sleepier you are. Hello, Mr. Reteau.

RETEAU

Hello, Miss Oliva.

OLIVA

Where is the Countess?

RETEAU

The Countess left, Miss.

OLIVA

Left without seeing me? And why this precipitous departure?

RETEAU

To escape a danger which threatens her and threatens you, at least as much.

OLIVA

A danger?

RETEAU

Yes. A matter of this officer—this Ship rigger.

OLIVA

The one we played the trick on in the Bathes of Apollo? Oh!
How distinguished he was—I've known lot of officers in my
life, but none as distinguished.

RETEAU

Exactly. It seems this one boasted of obtaining things from the
Queen.

OLIVA

Ah! That's not true! We were called back right away.

RETEAU

Whatever the case may be, the King's justice doesn't joke on
such a chapter, Madame. The Countess has taken the precaution of preparing your passage to England and from there to
America.

OLIVA

Mercy! But then, no more Palace Royale! No more Ball of the
Opera—no more Paris! Oh! No! No! That's impossible. I have
another way.

RETEAU

Which is—?

OLIVA

Go throw myself at the feet of the Queen! In short, I acted only
to please her, she won't refuse to protect me. As for the rest, I

am sure that will be the opinion of Mr. Beausire.

RETEAU

Beausire?

OLIVA

Yes! I didn't tell you. Ah! My word! I was too bored when I wrote him in secret to come fetch me away. And I would be very astonished if he wasn't here today.

RETEAU

Here.

(aside) In that case—not a moment to lose.

(aloud) Well, I'm delighted to hear it!

OLIVA

Really?

RETEAU

Yes, certainly! But your lunch is getting cold.

(pouring for her)

OLIVA

And there I was so afraid of being scolded.

RETEAU

But I would actually rather he was here, this dear Mr. Beausire, drinking his chocolate with you. I would say to him—

OLIVA

You would say to him—

(she raises the cup to her lip)

(Beausire's head appears above the wall.) Beausire, Great God—look—

(she lets her cup call and it breaks) Him!

(He jumps the wall and falls into her arms.)

BEAUSIRE

You! It's you.

OLIVA

At last!

(after embraces) Now let me present to you, Mr. Reteau de la Villette a friend of the Madame de la Motte-Valois—for you don't know it's in her place that I am.

BEAUSIRE

(after shaking Reteau's hand) Not possible! You will tell me all about this. We are going to leave.

OLIVA

Leave—for where?

BEAUSIRE

First of all for England and from there to America.

RETEAU

How things fall out.

(He goes out.)

OLIVA

Exactly as the Countess, who was pressing me to go meet her there.

BEAUSIRE

Well, let's hurry up. Make your preparations and let's leave.

OLIVA

You're in that much of a hurry?

BEAUSIRE

I should say so—

(aside) With such devils at my heels!

RETEAU

I've actually ordered a post chaise which will be here in a

moment.

(aside) The work will be crude but this proud arm doesn't worry me. I've mastered more formidable than his.

OLIVA

Why thinking about it—to make such a voyage—have you then become rich?

BEAUSIRE

(pulling a package of notes which he strews over Oliva's knees) Here! Look!

OLIVA

Lord! Where'd you earn all that?

BEAUSIRE

In an operation—on the Portuguese funds.

OLIVA

Ah! What luck! Fortune and love. Paradise on Earth! For I, too, I've got money.

BEAUSIRE

Truly!

(taken with scruples) It's not the price of dishonor at least?

OLIVA

Oh! What do you take me for? Keep it, you hold the cash!

RETEAU

(returning with Rosalie who brings a cloak hat and box) Here's your baggage.

BEAUSIRE

Let's go—make it quick.

OLIVA

I'm ready.

(Noise of bells—the top of a carriage appears behind the wall.)

RETEAU

I hear your carriage.

OLIVA

En route!

(She takes Beausire's arm and heads toward the gate. Behind the gate in front of the carriage Saint Landry and the Portuguese.)

PORTUGUESE

Pardon me!

SAINT LANDRY

Excuse me!

PORTUGUESE

You were expecting us, my dear Beausire?

SAINT LANDRY

Because you wouldn't leave, I am sure of it, without settling our little accounts.

BEAUSIRE

(stammering) Gentlemen—gentlemen.

(aside) My breath is cut off—

PORTUGUESE

You'll invite us to sit?

SAINT LANDRY

Very friendly—in truth.

(They sit.)

RETEAU

(to Oliva) What's this mean?

OLIVA

(to Reteau) I don't understand anything.

BEAUSIRE

Well, so be it—let's get it over with.

PORTUGUESE

We ask nothing better. We say that you have in trust for our association a sum of 108,000 pounds.

SAINT LANDRY

Which makes 36,000 francs for each of us.

BEAUSIRE

Of us three!

(sighing) Oh! Well! We have to let it go like that. Here's 72,000 francs.

OLIVA

Exactly!

SAINT LANDRY

You are the pearl of treasurers.

BEAUSIRE

I can then take leave of you, gentlemen, to the future.

PORTUGUESE

(stopping him) Yet one more word—for this money is not only destined for us, we are too honest to want to frustrate our associates.

SAINT LANDRY

And as these gentlemen have accompanied us here—

SAINT LANDRY

Here they are!

(They enter.)

PORTUGUESE

Still, it's fair, is it not to pay the expenses of their trip?

BEAUSIRE

Their expenses?

ALL

Hell—

BEAUSIRE

Yes—finally.

(sighing) And at how much do you set this figure?

SAINT LANDRY

It seem to me they are worth the sum of 36,000 pounds.

BEAUSIRE

(protesting) Why, gentlemen, what will remain to me?

PORTUGUESE

Exactly that which remained to ourselves.

SAINT LANDRY

Before having had the pleasure of knowing you.

(All smiles they've each trained a pistol on Beausire)

OLIVA

(terrified) Oh! No—no—not that! Do what these gentlemen want, darling.—who cares about the rest, since I am rich.

BEAUSIRE

(extending the last bundle, sighing) Here! It's written that I will never give money to women! Come, Oliva.

PORTUGUESE

Pardon! But Madame is staying.

BEAUSIRE

What are you saying?

SAINT LANDRY

That as for you, you are free but we have instructed to escort, Madame, a short distance from here to the Inn of the Crowned

Pharo—where we must deliver here into the hands of a gentleman on behalf of Mr. Count de Cagliostro.

PORTUGUESE

Our friend.

SAINT LANDRY

Who enlisted us.

RETEAU

Game's over. Let's get out of here.

BEAUSIRE

Ah! Indeed, never.

PORTUGUESE

Oh! Dear Mr. Beausire, you are going to force us to use methods we'd be desolate to use with you.

SAINT LANDRY

Come on, gentlemen, hand to the ladies.

OLIVA

Beausire, protect me.

(He gives a signal. Enter the Philosopher, L'artaigne, Le Grigneaux, the Commander and Positive in the tattered costumes of swordsmen—who throw themselves on him.)

BEAUSIRE

You will not touch this woman. She belongs to me—and to keep her, I am capable of anything—you hear anything!—even having courage!

(He is surrounded, disarmed and arms tied behind his back by three of the associates. The others have become masters of Oliva, who's fainted and they carry her to the carriage.)

SAINT LANDRY

Alas! Mr. Beausire—what could you expect to do against three?

CHARNY

(entering) The slander won't touch your face, my queen, and you can die under your royal mantle. Coachman—route to Paris.

**CURTAIN**

# ACT V

## SCENE 13: THE TWO QUEENS

*A square before the post house in Chailly, the last relay before Fontainbleau. At back to the left, the grilled gate of a park. Also on the left, the post house with the carriage doorway giving on stables and another giving on the interior. To the right, midstage, a pavilion. Further back, a wooden gate giving on the courtyard of the post office. Before the house on the right, rustic tables and chairs set against the house. In the middle at the rear—a stake with four arms indicating four roads. Panorama at the back. To the right, a park—allowing the village church of Chailly to be seen and at the rear, the trees of the Forest of Fontainbleau.*

*Cagliostro is seated in the front of the pavilion at the right. A sentinel is posted at the gate of the Court.*

CAGLIOSTRO

(to post-mistress) So it's actually here, actually, Madame, at the relay post from Chailly, where the carriages and the coach coming from Bar-sur-seine are stationed.

POST MISTRESS

Yes, sir—if you want horses, you'll have to wait for Her Majesty stopped here unexpectedly on her way to Fontainbleau and the master of the stables has requisitioned all our horses for their service.

CAGLIOSTRO

Oh! That doesn't matter much to me—I'm not leaving right way. Ah! Their Majesties are here?

POST MISTRESS

With all the Court, and at the moment, they are all lunching in my large hall. Ah! Sir, what a fine appetite the King has! Holy Virgin, how dear it must cost us to feed him.

CAGLIOSTRO

Yes, very dear.

POST MISTRESS

But there it is, heading the other way. I am going to serve in that little hall because these buildings and their appendages are reserved for Their Majesties.

CAGLIOSTRO

Indeed? That's very fair.

(Cagliostro and the Post Mistress leave. King and Court enter.)

KING

You say, Breteuil, that this Madame de la Motte-Valois has been arrested?

BRETEUIL

And she's here, sir, ready to appear before Your Majesty.

KING

(seeing Andrea enter) Ah! Miss de Taverney—have you informed the Queen?

ANDREA

Yes, sire, but Her Majesty does not wish to see the Countess de la Motte. She entreats the King to receive her, and if he wishes to satisfy the Queen, completely, to receive her before the entire Court.

KING

You heard, Breteuil. Stay, Miss de Taverney, the Queen is right. It's in broad daylight they must be confounded.

(the whole Court files in. At the back a detachment of Swiss Guards, with the Countess in their midst)

COUNTESS

(aside) By now Reteau has executed my orders. I am calm.

KING

(seated at the right) Ah! There you are at last, Madame. Where were you hiding?

COUNTESS

Me, hiding, Sire? If I'd been hiding, no one would ever have found me. I left Paris, that's all!

KING

And first of all, Do you know that Mr. de Rohan is in the Bastille?

COUNTESS

They told me so, Sire.

KING

You guess quite well, why?

COUNTESS

Me—not at all.

KING

Still, you know you spoke to the Queen of a diamond necklace proposing on behalf of the Cardinal, a means of paying for it.

COUNTESS

That's true, Sire.

KING

And then?

COUNTESS

And then, Her Majesty being unable to pay because the King had refused the money Mr. Calonne requested for her—she sent back the jewel box.

KING

By whom? And to whom?

COUNTESS

By me, to the Cardinal.

KING

And why to the Cardinal, if you please, instead of returning it to the jewelers?

COUNTESS

Because Cardinal de Rohan, being in agreement with the Queen in the matter, would have been injured not to have the opportunity to finish it himself as he had begun it.

KING

Cardinal de Rohan in agreement with the Queen? How could that happen, since for a long while the Cardinal has no longer had private access to Her Majesty—well—will you speak?

COUNTESS

I have nothing further to say, Sire, except before the Queen.

KING

The Queen has no intention of seeing you. After having shown you a kindness that she repents—the Queen is experiencing the scorn which she should always have felt—if she'd listened to me.

COUNTESS

I submit to the insults of my King—as for the Queen, having only carried out her orders, I cannot believe that today she would disavow me.

KING

The Queen's orders? Yet one more time, regarding what, Madame? If you have something to answer, speak. But no, you fear the scandal of a public admission—after having inflicted on your sovereign the scandal of public suspicion.

COUNTESS

You mean, Sire, on the contrary that I am holding my peace, so as to avoid any for the Queen.

KING

So, you are accusing the Queen?

COUNTESS

(hypocritically) I, Sire? And of what? If Her Majesty sees the Cardinal secretly, it's possibly because she has her reasons for that, and if others come to the question of accusing the Queen the idea certainly didn't come from me.

KING

And where would the Queen have seen the Cardinal, according to you?

COUNTESS

The first time at eleven o'clock in the evening, a week ago today, in the park opposite the Baths of Apollo. Yet again, I don't see any crime in the interviews between the Queen and the Cardinal, but I cannot prevent their taking place.

KING

The Queen denies them.

COUNTESS

Sire, I'm a Valois, the Cardinal is a Rohan—and we both affirm—

KING

Because the two of you are accomplices—but the judges will decide.

COUNTESS

You are right, Sire, the judges will decide if it is possible that the Cardinal, like myself—we were able to see them both—a woman dressed like the Queen saying the same words really being the Queen. For this it will have to be admitted that, I, like Cardinal de Rohan submitted at the same moment to the same and very unusual hallucination.

KING

(with severity) Or that in the Kingdom there exists a woman who resembles the Queen to the point of having distracted you as she had already distracted those who thought they saw her at the tub of Mesmer, scandalizing the idlers and the filles de joie.

COUNTESS

(loud) If such a miracle exists, Sire, why has Mr. de Crosne, who has his hand on all the police in the realm, not already indicated it? Why hasn't he put his grip on this mysterious twin? Such a resemblance could not pass unnoticed. Let the woman be found—and let them say to the judges as well as the Cardinal and myself—here she is!

CHARNY

(appearing with Oliva) Here she is!

COUNTESS

(terrified) Oliva!

OLIVA

(throwing herself at the King's feet)

KING

(looking at her) Great God!

CHARNY

Sire, Madame de la Motte-Valois insists she be shown this second Queen of France, who wasn't afraid to usurp an august and sacred place—but what she didn't say, was that the infamous one who maneuvered this ignorant girl into this sacrilege was she herself alone, and no one else.

COUNTESS

Fie! I don't know this woman!

OLIVA

You don't know me? Me that you came to find in the Palace Royale that you brought away, fed, dressed, styled. Ah! Madame, whom will you persuade of that?

KING

See this woman, all of you, intimates familiar with the Queen, and say if you would not have taken her for your sovereign?

MME DE POLIGNAC

Oh! Sire! This resemblance is terrifying.

ANDREA

Now I understand.

(aside) And there I was accusing her.

KING

Take your prisoner to the Queen, Mr. de Charny, before taking her to Madelonnettes so that sight of her will further prove to Her Majesty the unworthiness of the one to whom she had the weakness of granting her confidence.

(Oliva and Charny go out right.)

KING

And you, Madame, confess your crime, like that wretch, so the frankness of the confession and your repentance will be worth perhaps the indulgence of your judges.

COUNTESS

(furious) Sire, I repeat to you that I don't know that woman—she's a false witness suborned for my ruin—but ill luck to those who accuse me, for they intend to ruin me, I will dishonor them.

KING

Madame, take care!

COUNTESS

And you, too, take care, Sire. Take care that opinion not accuse the Queen of striking me down—not for guilt but for complicity. The throne of Kings is not so high that the voice of the people doesn't climb there.

KING

Let them take this wretch away. You pretend to descend from the Kings of France, Madame—well, the fleur de lys you are claiming, will come from the hand of my executioner who will give it to you!

COUNTESS

(as she's dragged off) Ah! Cowards! Cowards! Cowards who allow a daughter of their Kings to be tortured.

CHARNY

(entering) Sire, the Queen!

KING

Well, Madame, no matter what their audacity, your enemies are confounded.

QUEEN

(entering from the right) Thanks to Mr. de Charny.

KING

Don't worry, we will pay your debt!

QUEEN

(to Charny) Count, I cannot give you a more precious blessing than the fiancée who's going to be your wife. She is worthy of you—and you are worthy of her. Make her as happy as I am today. She deserves it even more than I do.

CHARNY

I promise to consecrate my whole life to making Miss de la Taverney happy.

ANDREA

(low to Queen) Ah! Madame—how you avenge yourself.

QUEEN

(low to Andrea) Like a friend, Andrea.

(at the back appears an escort of hussars to royal pikemen and the royal carriage)

VAUDREUIL

The carriage of Their Majesties awaits their good pleasure.

KING

Then on our way; you will take a seat in our carriage with your wife, Mr. de Charny.

CAGLIOSTRO

(to Charny as he passes by him) My compliments, Count—you are the hero of the day.

CHARNY

Thanks to you, sir.

CAGLIOSTRO

Yes! You served them today. Beware of tomorrow!

**CURTAIN**

# ABOUT THE AUTHOR

**Frank J. Morlock** has written and translated many plays since retiring from the legal profession in 1992. His translations have also appeared on Project Gutenberg, the Alexandre Dumas Père web page, Literature in the Age of Napoléon, Infinite Artistries. com, and Munsey's (formerly Blackmask). In 2006 he received an award from the North American Jules Verne Society for his translations of Verne's plays. He lives and works in México.